mindful
simplicity

mindful simplicity

Practical Strategies for Finding Harmony in Your Home, Work, and Life

Yolanda V Acree

ROCKRIDGE PRESS

Interior and Cover Designer: Michael Patti
Art Producer: Sara Feinstein
Editor: Lia Ottaviano
Production Editor: Chris Gage

Cover photography © Sophia Hsin/Stocksy.

All illustrations used under license from Shutterstock.com

ISBN: Print 978-1-64152-922-8 | eBook 978-1-64152-923-5

R0

This book
is dedicated to my mother, Althea, who unknowingly inspired me on this journey, and to all those aspiring to live simply.

Contents

Introduction

——

Welcome! My name is Yolanda and I'm going to be your guide through the process of simplifying your life. I'm so excited to be taking you on this journey. Simplicity is a tool I've been using for over six years to clear away the clutter in my own life and prioritize what matters most to me. I've also used this tool to help my family, friends, and people like you find contentment in their own lives.

Let's step back in time to when my life wasn't so simple. From the outside, my life probably looked great to others: I was supporting myself with a career I enjoyed, I was in a new relationship, I spent time with my friends and family regularly, and I had the ability to fulfill my physical needs and wants. Yet on the inside, something felt off. I didn't feel excited or even content about my life, the stuff around me wasn't giving me the joy I had hoped for, and I didn't have any goals or passions driving me.

At the time, I didn't understand what was wrong, but I knew I needed to do something. My motto and strategy at the time was "start where it's easy" to try to improve my situation, and where it was easy was all the stuff staring me in the face. I got rid of many things, including my job, that were standing between me and myself. When I was satisfied with what I had left, I could clearly see the life I had been living was not the one I really wanted. I now had the time and space to start figuring out what my priorities were.

Simplifying my life exposed me to the fact that I didn't even know what my values were. I had never taken the time to consciously consider what mattered to me. It also helped me understand the importance of doing work more closely aligned with my personal values and gave me the flexibility to pursue other interests, such as entrepreneurship and travel. I've also been teaching an introductory minimalism class, and I have the honor of leading a digital minimalist community of over 7,000 individuals.

I'm proud of what I have accomplished, but at the beginning of my journey, I could have used a book like this. In my opinion, I did the process backward. I decluttered and then I began to think about my values, priorities, and what simple living meant to me. Now, I advise my clients to first think about why they want to simplify their life and then work on the physical decluttering. Starting with your *why* helps you release unwanted items and situations mindfully. This book will help you do just that.

On this journey, you will learn what simplicity is, as well as how to apply it to every area of your life. Simplicity is a buzzword you've probably seen floating around online, so I will begin by clarifying what is meant when we talk about simplicity and the key approach to successfully practicing the art of simplicity: mindfulness. I'll break down what mindfulness is and how to use it to determine what your priorities are. Additionally, I'll give you practical and proven tips and strategies to easily incorporate simplicity into the main areas of your life.

The most common areas that folks report having difficulties simplifying are their homes, work spaces, family life, finances and budgeting, shopping, food and diet, relationships, and time management. We are going to explore the following areas together, starting at home:

- Within our homes, we often find clutter around books and paper, decor, and storage areas. In the *Home* chapter, you'll learn how to identify problem areas in your home that attract clutter and ways to incorporate your values into the life of your home, all while increasing order and functionality and adding more beauty and relaxation.
- Our jobs may already bring with them a certain amount of stress, so our goal in the *Office and Work Space*

chapter is to introduce clearing and organizational strategies that encourage productivity. We'll discuss how best to manage your files and calendar, evaluate how effectively you use your time, and design a work space that reflects your ethics and personality.

- Home and *Family Life* are naturally intertwined. Besides the physical home space, clutter can creep into our schedules, chores, and daily family routines. Here we'll work on developing an optimal environment where your family's physical and emotional needs can be prioritized and you can enjoy each other's company.

- *Finances and Budgeting* is another area that can be a source of stress and disorder. It's important to know where your money is going, how to manage your money, how to make it work for you and your goals, and how to use credit responsibly.

- Diving deeper into our *Shopping* habits, we take a closer look at what we buy and why. What motivates us to shop and what do our purchases reveal about us? In this chapter, you'll learn ways to shop more mindfully, particularly for items that you buy regularly, like clothing, food, and household supplies.

- In the next chapter, we'll talk about *Food and Diet* and how to simplify our eating habits. Being able to feed ourselves and our families with food that is fulfilling, healthy, and affordable is a top priority for many people. Additionally, strategies will be provided for organizing the kitchen to support the preparation and enjoyment of the meals you consume.

- We interact with many different groups of people in our lives, such as immediate and extended family, friends and acquaintances, coworkers, and significant others, both in person and in digital communities. In this chapter, we discuss how to prioritize the *Relationships* that matter most.

- *Time Management* is the final area we'll address and perhaps the most valuable because we need it to accomplish everything else in our lives. We'll consider what's on your personal schedule, where you may be wasting time, the importance of *you* time, and how to align your priorities with your time.

Having gained all these strategies to simplify and prioritize the most significant areas of your life, we'll weigh options and resources for implementing and maintaining the simplicity in your new, uncomplicated life. The process starts right now and, by the end of this book, you will never think about your life in the way same again!

Part 1

—

Living Simply

What does it mean to live simply? This section is all about understanding what simplicity is and how we can use it to improve our lives. Simplicity involves combining practical actions with mindful choices. We'll explore how simplifying our lives not only involves decluttering physical things, but also our minds.

Chapter 1

Your Simplicity Springboard

Every change you make in your life involves two parts: a choice and an action. The choices we make begin in our minds and influence the actions we take to fulfill that choice. Our goal in this chapter is to give you a strong working knowledge of mindful simplicity. We're also going to investigate the historical and psychological factors that impact our patterns of consumption as a society and as individuals, causing us to accumulate physical and mental clutter.

Simplicity: A Pathway to Freedom

Simplicity is what is left when all the excess and clutter in your life is cleared away. Simplicity is the art of adequately fulfilling our needs and desires with peace of mind, knowing they are in alignment with our values and who we are at our core. Simplicity is all of the small steps we can take to make our lives and the world around us more enjoyable. Practicing simplicity does not mean you will never have complications in your life again; it means you will have the knowledge and tools to willfully and appropriately address them.

Why did you pick up this book? I would bet it's because you've felt overwhelmed with the responsibilities on your plate, the piles of stuff around your home, work issues, navigating complex relationships, or some or all of the above. You probably know there's a simpler way to live a more balanced life and feel the joy you deserve, but it's felt out of reach or unrealistic for your situation. I'm here to tell you that simplicity, as we approach it, is doable and can give you the freedom and ease you crave. The concept of simplicity delves into the practical actions you can take to declutter and simplify your emotional and physical worlds, based on a mindful examination of your priorities and values.

Starting Where It's Easy

This idea of looking at clutter from a practical standpoint helped me greatly when I was starting my simplicity journey and it can help you, too. Part of our approach to simplicity is using realistic strategies to help you clear away the excess in your life. Small actions such as drinking a glass of water when you wake up, unsubscribing from junk mail, calling a family meeting, not eating lunch at your desk, or using the night setting on your phone can have a major impact on your daily life. In later chapters, we'll explore the simple actions you can take every day to mindfully minimize your distractions.

Simplicity Is Not Simple

Before we dive more deeply into mindful simplicity, I want to be clear that simplicity does not mean simple. This process will take effort and time. There will be moments when you fail, feel like quitting, or when you forget why you are simplifying your life. In life, as with this journey, there are natural highs and lows. Through it all, I want you to remember there are other people out there in the world, including myself, on this journey with you and you can revisit this book and start over as often as you need to.

Mindful Simplicity

Mindfulness is the practice of being present with yourself. When you are mindful, you are aware of your thoughts, feelings, and senses. You are not dwelling in the past or the future, but are focused on the moment at hand. Practicing mindfulness allows us to be intentional about the choices we make and the actions we take, and it can be employed in any situation. It teaches us to acknowledge what we are experiencing in any given moment and then accept that reality so we can consciously act to change, if necessary. Mindfulness is also an important tool for understanding our values and having clarity about our priorities and goals. When we are focused on what matters most, we can apply our personal standards to the present experience and react purposefully.

Our ability to be mindful impacts all areas of our lives: what we consume, the ways we address problems, how we spend our time, our relationships with others, how we achieve our goals, and more. The great thing about mindfulness is that it starts within us. You don't need anything outside of you in order to be mindful. You simply need a desire to be aware.

Why do we need mindful simplicity? Why do we consume as we do? The answer is that we in the United States (and other western countries with capitalist economies) live in a culture that thrives on our desires and the ability to fulfill those desires. This culture did not emerge overnight, and it has been developing for centuries. Our culture of consumption is profoundly embedded in our minds and behaviors, so any strategies we employ to combat consumerism and materialism and simplify our lives must begin in the mind. It's important for us to understand how and why we got here.

The Roots of Our Consumerism

Let's take a peek into recent history to understand how we ended up with our current culture of consumption and our economic model. *The Encyclopedia Britannica* notes that the system of capitalism emerged in the sixteenth century in Europe and eventually spread farther west during the Age of Exploration. Capital, accumulated goods, assets, possessions, and so on became the main component of production. Naturally, those who could afford to acquire significant capital to produce goods for the market were usually wealthy, which created other problems, such as income inequality.

In the second half of the twentieth century, the growth of American consumerism took off. World War II spurred production booms and companies looked for ways to keep people spending. These strategies included tying patriotism ("Your country needs your support!") and the idea of the *American dream* (material prosperity and success available to all) to consumption. According to the Bureau of Labor Statistics, household incomes rose substantially, unemployment rates dropped, and our consumption has steadily increased each decade since the 1950s. Additionally, in this time period, education levels rose, gender roles began to shift, and policies of segregation ended, all of which opened the door to the market for many people who lacked access before. This time period is when we started to intensify our patterns of consumption and strengthen the association between our perceived worth and the things we own.

In fact, there is a term for the connection between the purchases we make and our self-worth: *compensatory behavior*. Sometimes we consume things to balance or improve our self-esteem and self-image, or what Dr. Johnathan Levav, marketing professor at Stanford University, calls *self-discrepancy*. In their 2016 study, featured on

InSight by Stanford Business, Levav and his co-authors found there were primarily five categories of compensatory behavior: direct resolution, an effort to solve a discrepancy or problem directly; symbolic self-completion, an effort to signal a desired identity; dissociation, avoiding unwanted associations; escapism, using consumption to distract yourself; and fluid compensation, consuming in a different domain that highlights your strengths. Although there are many reasons why we engage in this behavior, we as individuals are not always aware we are doing so and each person's motivations vary. Combine our compensatory behavior with marketing and the obstacles we're facing start to become clear.

How We Consume

Marketing is a set of psychological tactics used to encourage Americans to consume. Because the free market is driven by supply and demand, consumers should ideally determine the demand for products based on their needs and desires. However, in our current market, companies create the demand for products by spending millions on marketing, including advertising, to get you to buy their products. The marketing tactics used at the turn of the twentieth century were considered revolutionary in those times. However, in the twenty-first century, there are much more sophisticated methods at play. Thanks to the introduction of the Internet and other electronic technologies and vast improvements in transportation and logistics, we now have unprecedented access to goods and services. The Internet changed two major things for us: the way we shop and how we access our money. Online commerce, in addition to social media, has fueled our culture of instant gratification.

We are bombarded with advertising everywhere, including our mailbox, inbox, television, radio, billboards, magazines, newspapers, and, most recently, our social media and other mobile applications. Additionally, we have companies such as Amazon, which offer one-click ordering and same-day delivery. Credit and debit cards, payment apps such as PayPal and Cashapp, and other types of installment credit accounts have created a cashless society that makes it easier to get credit and accumulate a lot of stuff quickly, much of which we don't really need or want, though we've convinced ourselves we do.

Evolving technology and social media have not only impacted how we consume, but also how we relate to each other. We have so many methods to stay connected to one another in the digital age, but it has also, ironically, created a culture of disconnection. We tend to fill emotional voids from lack of real-time connection to people with devices and other objects. Technology has also changed the way we work, giving employers more access to employees outside of traditional work hours and providing more people with opportunities to work from home, which can impact family life. We are busier than ever, filling our days with work and activities and our nights with media-streaming apps. Instead of saving us time, technology has increasingly stolen it. Yet, some people wear their "busy-ness" as a badge of honor. Social media encourages this dangerous phenomenon. "If you didn't post it, did it really happen?" is a popular phrase in today's technology-driven culture. We are burned-out in every way possible and it's time to make a change toward a more peaceful and simple existence.

In examining burnout culture, we likewise need to consider how we are defining success. If the prevailing attitudes in American culture define success as the attainment of objects and the glorification of being busy, disguised as productivity, what does the desire to simplify say about us? Does it mean we are lazy and idle if we want easier days, less work, more leisure time with our loved ones, and more self-care for ourselves? I think we are finally realizing the vision of success we have been sold is not enough. What does success mean to you? We can no longer assume that society's definition of success applies to us. We have to redefine this concept and many others for ourselves. Success can look and feel like whatever we want it to, including simplicity.

This is why mindful simplicity is so meaningful. Mastering mindful simplicity can mean the difference between thriving in a fulfilling life and just continuing to survive another day. Our minds are powerful but are also driven by routines and subconscious influences, such as marketing techniques and societal cues. The mind is the battleground in our efforts to create simple lives. We have to push through all we've been taught about our worth and value, consumption, and success to live the lives we truly want. Mindful simplicity, along with taking simple actions, is the tool to change our way of living.

The Things That Take Up Space

All types of clutter, mental and physical, crowd our lives and we may not even know all of it is there. It's typically easier to see the physical clutter in our homes and other spaces because the stuff is in our way, but the mental clutter is much more subtle. Let's look at some of the physical and mental obstacles to simplicity.

PHYSICAL CLUTTER

The clichés "more is better" and "bigger is better" explain the real source of our physical clutter. The following statistics based on the past few years of consumption in the United States illustrate how expensive clutter is in our lives:

- *Forbes* reported the average home size has more than doubled since 1950 when the consumption boom began, and *Insurify* reported that sport utility vehicles have increasingly become the transportation of choice for many Americans because of their spaciousness. Therefore, our living spaces and our vehicles have gotten roomier to accommodate our stuff.
- Americans spent approximately $40 billion on storage facilities in 2018 according to AARP. In addition to storing items in our closets, drawers, cabinets, sheds, garages, and attics, we are paying companies to rent us more storage space off-site, away from our primary homes.

- Clutter has become so overwhelming that people pay extraordinary sums just to organize it. The organization industry was approaching $1 billion in revenue in 2015, as reported by *Forbes*. This includes professionals who offer in-home and in-office organizing services, as well as companies that sell do-it-yourself storage solutions.
- The American Cleaning Institute reported that we spent nearly $60 billion on cleaning supplies and services in 2016. Laundry and dry cleaning, dishwashing, housekeeping, detailing, steam cleaning, and other services are required to regularly maintain the stuff we own.

These facts are just the tip of the clutter iceberg. Fast fashion has drowned us in clothing that is cheaply made and disposable, and the increase in subscription clubs that deliver products to our doors monthly without us having to give a second thought has our containers overflowing with products. Sadly, even as some of us try to clean out our spaces and make room, thanks in part to the tidying-up movement originated by Marie Kondo back in 2014, even thrift shops, charity organizations, and consignment stores are reaching their capacity for accepting our used items, according to the *Wall Street Journal*. We really have no more space for our physical clutter, not to mention the negative impact our consumption is having on the environment.

MENTAL CLUTTER

Mental clutter is much more insidious than physical clutter. It creeps into the crevices of our minds and manifests itself in strange ways. Just as our spaces are filled to the brim, so are our heads. In fact, our physical clutter actually contributes to our mental clutter. Have you ever felt like you couldn't focus because the area around you was messy or disorganized? While some people say they thrive in chaos, I believe the vast majority of us prefer clean and clear spaces to relax and think. We have never-ending to-do lists for home and work, notifications and signals from our electronics, and obligations and expectations in our relationships. All of these stimuli keep our brains spinning, and it can feel like we never get a break. How often do you declutter your mind? Do you even know how to declutter your mind?

Mental clutter brings emotional and physical symptoms. It can show up as stress, anxiety, exhaustion, headaches, depression, boredom, body aches, forgetfulness, and procrastination. What do Americans worry about most? Not surprisingly, accumulating more things isn't at the top of this list, yet we can't escape the consequences of the things we buy. We also often experience stress when we have to work hard to afford our basic living expenses, transportation, education, retirement funds, and leisure time. Furthermore, we often complain that we never have enough time to get everything done, which produces more anxiety. And what about our personal time? Getting a haircut, scheduling wellness appointments, sleeping, or taking ourselves out on a date all demand time we are running short on. In addition to taking care of ourselves, we often have others who depend on us for their physical and emotional needs, such as our children, partners, parents, or pets. We also have social responsibilities to our families, friends, and coworkers. All of this uses up our mental capacity and can impact how we process information and make decisions on a daily basis.

When our relationships are unhealthy or complicated, that introduces more clutter into an already full mind. How we communicate with people can also introduce more mental junk that we have to wade through. We aren't just using social media to keep in touch with loved ones, but we are also endlessly scrolling to stay informed, to be entertained, to shop, and to compare ourselves to others, whether we are aware of it or not. Studies cited by *Psychology Today* have shown using social media can produce feelings of jealousy, inadequacy, and depression. Seeing positive images and posts of your friends can trigger you to have negative feelings about yourself, particularly if you're already in a bad mood.

Similar to online environments, our physical environments can cause mental clutter. Does your home reflect who you are? Do you feel you have enough space to relax, entertain, and live without feeling crowded? How do you feel about the town or city you live in? Do you feel comfortable and safe in your surroundings? Do you feel you have room to grow and explore in your environment? Is everything that you need and want easily accessible? How is the waste and pollution managed in your city? These are situations that can cause additional stress and impact your mental health.

THE SOURCE OF JOY

Physical and mental clutter can steal our joy and trick us into believing we have nothing to be grateful for. Joy comes when we are in alignment with our values and goals and when we feel our lives are abundant. When our *why* matches what we need and want, what is healthy and fulfilling, and our behavior and surroundings, we experience bliss. That is the goal of mindful simplicity.

How This Book Will Help

I've presented a lot of information throughout this chapter, not to overwhelm you, but hopefully to help you grasp the gravity of this issue. As a nation, we are facing a crisis, but we have the power to work through it together and improve our well-being. History is only doomed to repeat itself if we fail to learn the lessons. It has been clearly demonstrated that our patterns of consumption and cohabitation over nearly a century have been harmful to our wallets, psyches, and environments. We now have the knowledge and insight to make better choices, and this book will serve as our guide as we begin.

You're not alone on this journey. Remember, I am here to help guide you through this process of simplifying your life. I have been where you are standing before and know the challenges of making great changes. I also know the power of making small, consistent, and impactful changes over time. I want you to be prepared in knowing change takes time. You're not going to simplify your life overnight. You have spent years, if not decades, forming the habits that have cluttered and complicated your life, and it may take years to undo those practices and create new routines. It may also take time for your partner, children, friends, roommates, and others to come on board with some consistent modeling and encouragement. Regardless, these ideas and techniques are practical enough that you can start implementing them immediately, either on your own or with others.

This book is your practical companion and contains enough actionable strategies you can put to use right now to get started down the road to simplicity. Chapters 1 and 2 should be read first to get you settled in and comfortable with deciding on your *why*—what you value, what your priorities are, and what is best for you. The following eight chapters can be read in any order and are full of applicable tips and exercises to simplify the major areas of your life.

The final chapter contains tips to help you continue living a life of simplicity until making mindful choices becomes second nature. Finally, you own this book, so you can always refer back to it whenever you need a refresh or are having challenges. Think of it as your personal springboard to simplicity.

The task may seem insurmountable when you think about everything you have to simplify, but you have the strength and the tools to change your life through mindful choices. In the next chapter, we will dive into understanding and identifying your priorities, which will assist you in consciously choosing what is best for you and avoiding those influences that seek to keep you trapped in the cycle of clutter.

Chapter 2

Simple Priorities

An important part of making mindful choices is understanding your priorities. We can't streamline our lives without being aware of what matters most to us. In this chapter, you will take time to think about what is actually important to you. Once you have a thorough appreciation of your priorities, you will be able to complete a fundamental exercise to list your top three priorities for each of the eight areas you plan to simplify. This exercise will be essential as you work through the strategy chapters. Finally, we'll learn about staying present in this process, which is crucial to practicing mindful simplicity while attending to your priorities.

Understanding Your Priorities

We've learned a lot about the reasons we as a society have issues with consumption and clutter, which is largely due to a history of capitalist practices, influential marketing strategies, and the meshing of self-worth and possessions. Now, it's time to get a little more personal about the reasons you're reading this book. We can't talk about priorities without knowing why you're here. You need to know how you got here and why you're ready to make a change now. In thinking about your personal story, it's important to be very honest with yourself. No one is judging you, and this information will help you as you complete the rest of this chapter and part 2 of this book. Take a few minutes to think about your journey to simplicity. Sometimes it's difficult to remember how we arrived at this moment because we've suppressed the unpleasant truths about the current state of our lives.

Priorities are those things that take precedence over all others. Your priorities are met before anything else and they are the norms on which you will not compromise. Establishing your values makes it easy to identify and name your priorities. For example, if you value your health, then you have to ask yourself, "How do I maintain my health?" You might answer, "By exercising regularly." This then becomes your priority. Because you value your health, you will ensure that you get physical activity done before other lesser tasks. You can also think of priorities by asking yourself, what do I need to do *now* to live my values? Priorities focus on the present moment, which is why knowing your priorities is critical to practicing mindful simplicity. Mindfulness allows us to keep our priorities at the forefront of our minds, and when you're actively aware of your priorities it is easy to make the right choices and act accordingly.

Another aspect of understanding your priorities is learning how to clear your mind so you can contemplate the things that matter. Having some tried-and-true techniques to easily access a peaceful state is key to allowing your priorities to emerge. Some simple ways to clear your mind and open the path for simplicity are deep breathing for several minutes, journaling about your day, or taking a short walk. Try these suggestions or find what is most effective for you in order to focus. Clearing your mind is an essential step in making mindful choices.

How many decisions do you make in a day? According to a Cornell University study from 2007, a person makes, on average, more than 200 choices about food alone on a daily basis, so we can guesstimate that we make thousands of conscious and subconscious choices every day. In fact, we have so many options to consider and decisions to make daily that many suffer from *decision fatigue*. The phenomenon is characterized by people depleting their mental energy as they make more and more decisions throughout the day. As they become more fatigued, they make poorer choices that are irrational and impulsive, are more likely to display irritation and anger when interacting with others, or shut down and do nothing at all, according to *New York Times* writer and author John Tierney. Now imagine what is happening in your brain as you peruse Instagram or while walking through a shopping mall, especially after a long day of work or errands. How much willpower do you have at any given moment to ensure you're making choices that are aligned with your priorities?

Take a moment to think about some of the decisions you've made recently, especially concerning the areas covered in this book: home, work, finances, family, food, shopping, relationships, and time management. How did you go about making these decisions? Did you create a plan, go over your options, or ask others for advice? What time of the day do you make the most important decisions?

I want you to consider not only the choices you have made, but also how you have made them. The process of making a decision is just as important as the decision itself. What were the driving forces behind those choices? A number of internal factors influence our decisions, such as our current feelings, past experiences, biases, demographics, a sense of urgency, and personal relevance, according to studies cited by the *Inquiries Journal*. Physiology—how our bodies function—impacts our choices too, such as when we make a decision when hungry. Some external factors influencing our decisions are our relationships with others, finances, the media, and our environment. We have less, if any, power over some of these factors, so it's a good idea to learn how to control the way we respond to them in order to lessen their potential negative impact.

Although many decisions are driven by factors that we are unaware of or can't control, we do have the power to change the methods we use to make choices by being conscious of our priorities and employing mindful simplicity. The more you live in agreement with your priorities and values, the simpler your life becomes. When you live in harmony, you can make judgment calls and problem-solve easily without stress, doubt, or the need for external confirmation.

Identifying Your Priorities

Now that you know the importance of priorities and the factors that affect decision-making, you can confidently identify your priorities. Being able to identify your priorities decreases the time, brainpower, and resources spent on nonessential problems and tasks. Instead of making 200 decisions about food per day, what if you only made 20 choices? Think about what else you could be doing with your time and energy when your life is prioritized. While identifying your priorities, you will also learn to identify and remove the distractions that intrude on your mindfulness. Mindfulness and prioritizing work together to help you shed unnecessary belongings, commitments, habits, and mind-sets. Knowing your priorities will help you distinguish between what is a need and a want, what is important now and what can wait.

Understanding the difference between what is important versus what is urgent will help you prioritize and organize your decisions and tasks. What is urgent or perceived as needing to be addressed promptly is not always important. What is important, a priority, doesn't always need to be addressed in the moment and may require time for consideration. According to Eisenhower, a tech company focused on task management tools, former president Dwight D. Eisenhower developed a formula for categorizing urgent and important judgments, called the *Eisenhower Matrix*. He divided urgent and important tasks into four sections: urgent and important, important and not urgent, urgent and not important, and not important and not urgent. Important and time-sensitive concerns should be resolved first. Important situations that are not time-sensitive can be scheduled for a more suitable time. Decisions that are time-sensitive but not important can be delegated, and activities that are neither time-sensitive nor important can be eliminated. Keep this methodology in the back of your mind as you name your priorities and think through the strategies presented in the subsequent chapters.

Using a system, whether it is the *Eisenhower Matrix* or another, simplifies the ongoing process of naming your priorities, giving you the space to fully appreciate what is present in your life. Whether it's your relationships, your home, or your health, when you remove the things that don't matter and home in on your priorities, you can clearly see the value and meaning these things bring to you. Being grateful produces more positive effects that will encourage you in your practice of mindful simplicity.

Combine gratitude with mindfulness and you have the perfect recipe for a simple, happy life. Mindfulness keeps you centered on your needs and priorities, while gratitude keeps you centered on appreciating what you currently have.

Centering your priorities also signals to others that you value yourself. It lets them know you are investing in yourself by simplifying your life and living mindfully. When the people in your life can see the changes you're making and that your priorities have narrowed, they understand how to better interact with you. You will still need to have conversations with those you encounter about your simplified lifestyle, but acting in line with your priorities primes the tone of your relations. Additionally, naming your priorities and living your values acts as an indirect accountability system. Those you are in relationships with may notice the differences and inquire about why you are making these changes, giving you an opportunity to explain, educate, and be an example to those you care about.

On top of improving your interactions with others, living in alignment reduces the stress, frustration, and pain associated with leading an unprioritized life. Think about how many situations have turned chaotic because you didn't know your priorities. Consider the physical effects of being stressed and frustrated, such as headaches, stomachaches, and high blood pressure. You owe it to your mental and physical health to clear the clutter, identify your priorities, and commit to them.

Finally, I want you to understand that your priorities can change over time as life's circumstances change. What's a priority today may not be a priority six months to a year from now. The priorities you choose in this chapter's exercise are what you want to focus on and prioritize at this time in your life. Priorities can be either short-term or long-term. As you name your priorities in the next section, you may also want to notate the priority's longevity. Mindful simplicity encourages flexibility and adaptability so that we can continue to meet our priorities, even as they evolve.

The Power of Staying Present

Perhaps the most important takeaway from this book after naming your priorities, and the precursor to all the strategies presented in part 2, is the act of remaining present as often as possible. No matter what's going on at any second, if you can master staying present and focusing on the now, you can do anything in your life. The past is gone and we can't change it, but hopefully, we've learned the lessons we

Naming Your Priorities

We've done a lot of work in the first two chapters to understand mindful simplicity and our priorities. Now it's time to designate your top three priorities for each area of your life. Space has been provided below for you to write your priorities. Use the suggestions from the previous section and work through your priorities thoughtfully. Remember, you will use these priorities to guide you as you learn the strategies to simplify each life area, so take as much time as necessary to settle on the top priorities you feel are relevant and aligned to your current values.

HOME: _____

CAREER: _____

FAMILY LIFE: _____

FINANCES: _____

SHOPPING: _____

FOOD AND DIET: _____

RELATIONSHIPS: _____

TIME MANAGEMENT: _____

How was the exercise? What was easy? What was challenging? Take a few moments to sit with your responses. This exercise alone has the power to create a huge shift in your mind-set and your life, and we haven't even gotten to the strategies yet! If you're having trouble naming your priorities, you can always revisit the "Understanding Your Priorities" section. It can be difficult if this is your first attempt at consciously identifying your priorities. Remember, part of being mindful is giving yourself enough time to process and acknowledge your feelings, so don't worry if it takes a bit more energy than you anticipated. Simply being present in this activity is an accomplishment.

need to continue our journey in the present. The future has yet to happen and we have no control over it. We expect our present actions will positively impact our futures, but the truth is we don't know what will happen with any certainty. Focusing on the past or future can cause worry and anxiety, which produces mental clutter, and mental clutter prevents us from centering our priorities and living simply. All we can control is the moment we're in right now.

The privilege of staying present is that it affords us space, something we all want in our quest for simplicity. We want the space to breathe, to think, to just *be*. This space is where our priorities are clear and our dreams and goals can be actualized. In this space, time is inconsequential. We can slow down, be still, and know without a doubt what matters. Another benefit of being in this space is that we're able to approach the uncomfortable situations with calm, ultimately reducing the discomfort of future difficult circumstances. Finally, staying present teaches us the power of acceptance. There are things we will not be able to change in our lives and for those things, acceptance is necessary. The practice of surrender allows us to grow through challenges and move forward with grace. Taking advantage of this power is a strategy you cannot afford to ignore as it will increase the effectiveness of the other strategies. Utilizing the power of staying present requires daily practice until it becomes natural. Whenever you're faced with a situation where it's difficult to stay present, here are some questions to ask yourself:

- *What is one thing I can do right now to change my situation?* Taking one step opens the pathway to the next. Even a small action can produce a great shift so that you can recenter yourself.
- *What emotions am I experiencing right now*? Accepting your feelings is key to staying tuned in. Your feelings are valid and are important signals that assist you in identifying different types of emotional, mental, and physical triggers. You don't have to react to your emotions to acknowledge them.
- *What do I see, smell, taste, hear, and feel?* Engaging our physical senses can bring us back to the present moment.
- *Am I reacting to what is happening right now or allowing my past experiences to affect my response?* Similarly, am I focused on the current moment or worrying about what could happen in the future? Remember that living in the past or future will likely create anxiety and unrealistic expectations, when what we want is peace and courage to exist in the present moment.

Another resource you may find useful for learning about staying present is one of my favorite books, *The Power of Now* by Eckhart Tolle. This worldwide best seller approaches the power of presence from a spiritual perspective, but the insights he reveals can be applicable for anyone, regardless of religious affiliation. For more information about *The Power of Now*, visit EckhartTolle.com or check for the book at your local library.

In part 1 of this book, we covered several concepts that highlight the importance of living simply, clutter-free, and aligned with our priorities. You now have the foundation you need to operate from a place of mindful simplicity, including an examination of the historical factors which have affected our consumption over the last century and current statistics about our clutter and consumption habits in the twenty-first century. We then got clear about our priorities, understanding their purpose, essentialness, and how to identify them. Additionally, you've learned the first and most important strategy to have with you always, which is the power of presence. In part 2, we will move into the strategies you can implement in conjunction with the priorities you have named. These strategies will assist you in creating a plan for simplifying each area of your life.

Part 2

—

Strategies for Living Simply Every Day

In the second section of this book we will learn practical tips for how to live simply. Now that you understand the importance of living mindfully to simplify your life and are aware of your top priorities, you can begin to implement these simple strategies to streamline your life. Each chapter will cover the main challenges of life when it comes to clutter and provide you with actionable techniques to eliminate that clutter.

Chapter 3

—

Home

Our homes are perhaps the most important spaces we occupy and the spaces where we spend the most time. When creating a simplified life, starting with your home is essential to setting the tone for your new journey.

Strategies for Simplifying Your Home

In chapter 2, you named your top three priorities for your home life. Take a moment to recall those priorities and, if it's helpful, make a few notes about those priorities on the lines below. As you read through the strategies for creating a simple home, keep your *why* and your values in mind as you consider how they can help you meet those priorities. Finally, remember to stay present as you apply these strategies to your life.

_____

_____

_____

Addressing Clutter in Your Home

Conducting a home evaluation will prepare you for the task of decluttering. The following strategies will ask you to critically assess your home needs and where your priorities and values fit into your space. You will find a similar section at the beginning of each chapter's strategy list. This activity can be done alone, with your partner, or with family. Some of the following questions may also evoke helpful information during the *Family Life* chapter.

- **Evaluate the size of your home.** Include all rooms where your stuff lives and don't forget auxiliary spaces such as attics, garages, and sheds. If you have home goods or personal items stored off-site in a storage facility or at a loved one's home, note where those items are located. What is the primary function of each space? What are the main activities that take place in those spaces? Think about how you use each space now and how you hope to use it in the future when it's clutter-free.

- **Assess who lives in your home.** Include each person's age, gender, and activities such as work, school, sports, and exercise. Make a note of their hobbies, such as video gaming or crafting. Don't forget about your pets. What are the mental and emotional needs of each person? Who enjoys and needs time alone to feel at peace and who prefers more time with others? Does anyone have mental health concerns? What are the personality traits of each person?

- **Appraise the material needs of each person.** How much and what types of clothing does each person need (clothing for work or fitness, uniforms for school or sports)? Does anyone have any physical health concerns or disabilities? Think about each person's activities and hobbies. Do they need equipment or supplies? Where and how does everyone sleep? If family members share a bedroom, how do you accommodate multiple people?

• **Use this information to plan for your space.** The findings compiled from these questions will help you review how you're utilizing the space in your home and the objects occupying those spaces. Keep a running, categorized list of what you need to meet the mental and physical needs of each person and space in your home as you declutter.

Removing Clutter

Physically removing clutter from your home is an essential part of the total simplification process. First, eliminating clutter frees up mental space. In chapter 1, we discussed how physical clutter contributes to mental clutter, making it difficult for us to think and relax in messy spaces. You will actually be able to think more clearly when your clutter is not staring you in the face. Secondly, removing the clutter from your home decreases the possibility that you or a family member will have second thoughts about keeping items you chose to discard. Resources for removing clutter are also provided at the end of this book.

- **Recycle.** You will need to do a little research on your city or county's recycling policies and local centers, but you should be able to recycle some of your unwanted materials. Electronics will likely need to go to a separate facility, or you can contact your nearest electronics store about their recycling program.

- **Donate.** If you have items in good or like-new condition, you can take them to your local thrift or charity organizations. If possible, it's best to drop off when a staff person is available to receive your donations and sort through the items. There was an influx of donations nationwide at the beginning of 2019 when the *Tidying Up with Marie Kondo* Netflix series was released, so it's courteous to speak with the organization first about what they have the capacity to accept and not just leave your stuff for them to sort out and toss if they can't use it.

- **Toss.** If an item is too damaged or not recyclable, it should be thrown away. Again, check your locality's waste policies for what types of items can be disposed of with the regular waste collection. Large or unusual items that you cannot place on the curb may need to be taken to the dump. You could also put "free" signs on items you want gone or list them on social media as free with a deadline to pick up.

- **Sell or trade.** If you have a Facebook account, you can sell your items locally via Facebook Marketplace and in your local Swap and Sell groups. You can also have a yard sale. Consignment shops will sell your items for you and take a percentage of the sale for their services. If you have vintage or high-value items, you may want to consider visiting your nearest pawn shop or antique dealer. From my personal experience selling items, it can take weeks or months. If you're not comfortable with potentially holding on to your undesirables for an extended period of time, I would suggest recycling, donating, or tossing.

- **Keep a clutter box available.** You can place it near a wastebasket or next to a frequently used exit point in your home. For ongoing maintenance, instruct your household members to place unwanted items they come across in it as everyone continues to declutter. When the box is full, decide how you will remove the items using the methods above.

Discarding Paper Clutter

Paper comes from everywhere. The mail is delivered six days per week and most people probably receive at least a couple of pieces of mail daily. The US Postal Service delivers 188 million pieces of first-class mail daily, not including priority and other special types of correspondence. We bring papers home from school, work, and appointments and have accumulated piles of important papers and receipts saved from years past. If you have a magazine subscription, you probably have stacks of them around your living space too. We also tend to leave papers wherever there are flat surfaces, like the kitchen table, coffee table, or nightstand, and in drawers, cabinets, and on shelves. In addition to paper, our electronic inboxes fill up too. Paper and e-mails are some of the fastest sources of clutter we collect, but there are easy ways to reduce them.

- **Stop the junk mail.** Circulars, flyers, credit card offers, and other unsolicited offers can build up quickly in a matter of weeks. You can call 1-888-567-8688 or go to the website OptOutPrescreen.com to opt out for five years or permanently. Doing this greatly reduced my snail mail to only a few pieces per week.

- **Go paperless.** Many companies you have accounts with, such as your bank or utility provider, may give you the option to receive electronic statements each month via e-mail. Check the companies' websites or give them a call to see if this is an option. If you use the physical statement as a reminder to pay, you can easily create a reminder on your digital calendar instead.

- **Establish a designated area for your mail.** Keep a paper shredder or a trash bin nearby. Immediately shred or tear up any unwanted mail and recycle or toss it. This stops the mail from migrating to other places in your home to pile up.

- **Establish another area to secure important documents that need to be saved.** You can scan important documents and pieces of mail for safe-keeping. If you don't have a scanner at home, you can download a scanning app to your smartphone or use the scanning feature on the Notes app if you're an iPhone user.

- **Create a physical inbox and outbox.** After you've shredded or discarded the junk mail, place important mail that needs to be reviewed in the inbox. Place any mail that needs to go out, such as bill payments or letters, in the outbox. This practice will prevent important notices from being forgotten.

- **Declutter your e-mails.** In addition to paper mail, you also receive similar types of e-mails in your inbox. If you don't check your e-mail regularly or have multiple accounts, you could have hundreds or thousands of e-mails to sort through. Pick a day or a few to sort through your inbox, discarding unwelcome e-mails and categorizing those that remain. You can use labels such as "bills," "online purchases/receipts," and "work," to organize them. Unroll.me is a free e-mail management service that helps you maintain a clean inbox.

Decorating Your Home Intentionally

As we declutter and redesign our space to reflect our simplified lives, it's important we still showcase our personality and values. Once you declutter, your home doesn't have to have the popular minimalist aesthetic of black-and-white decor and lots of negative space, unless, of course, it's your preferred aesthetic. You probably already have items in your home that can be repurposed and put on display.

- **Display your favorite books.** Books can double as personal items and home décor, and they can be difficult for many people to give up. Keep the ones you truly love to revisit and donate the ones you no longer need to your local library, schools, and charity organizations. Also remember that you can borrow books from your library that you're interested in but don't necessarily need to own. For the ones you choose to keep, find a special way to incorporate them with your existing decor. You can place them on a coffee table or shelf, for example.

- **Swap your decor.** If you have friends or neighbors who are also looking to eliminate clutter and update their home's style, coordinate a decor swap. It's an easy way to get new items without spending any money. You can all choose new decor pieces from each other's old stuff and what isn't selected can be tossed or donated after the party. It's an opportunity to spend some quality time with your friends and make the simplification process fun.

- **Minimize the colors.** Take a tour around your home, looking at all your furniture, curtains, lamps, bedding, and so on and observe what colors are present. Choose two or three colors that are consistent throughout your home, including at least one neutral color, and keep all the decor items that fall within that color scheme. Eliminate any items that don't match.

This will simplify your home visually and create consistency from room to room.

- **Eliminate seasonal decor and knickknacks.** We tend to collect these around holidays and birthdays and from past vacations. They can easily pile up and become clutter on our tables, on our shelves, and in our storage areas. For the seasons and holidays, choose one or two main items that represent what is special about that time for you and your family—or, in lieu of items, do something simple but meaningful to acknowledge the season. For example, you could go on a nature walk at the beginning of winter and collect a few pine cones to display in a bowl on your kitchen table, or you could share with your loved ones why you are thankful for your freedom on the Fourth of July.

- **Rearrange your furniture.** This is a great way to refresh the energy in your home. Assuming that you've removed any unnecessary pieces already, give each room a new layout. Leave some space between the walls and your furniture where possible to open up the flow, and keep windowpanes and sills as clear as possible to let the maximum light in. While you're rearranging the furniture, this is also a great time to give each room a good cleaning.

Decluttering Storage Spaces

Storage areas are where we put the clutter we don't want to think about or use on a daily basis. It's easy to forget about the things we have hidden away. Because many storage areas such as attics, garages, sheds, and off-site facilities are out of sight and mind, clutter builds up quickly year after year. Addressing your storage areas could be challenging, but it's necessary in order to prevent long-term clutter buildup.

- **Declutter all storage spaces seasonally.** Set a time at the end or beginning of each season to clean out all storage spaces. With this schedule, you can gradually reduce clutter without being overwhelmed. You can also maintain what is stored once all spaces have been sufficiently purged.
- **Discard any damaged or broken items.** Appliances and equipment take up a great deal of space naturally, so if it can't be used, discard it immediately. If the items were meaningful or needed, you would have repaired or replaced them by now.
- **Label all storage containers clearly.** Arrange the labeled side facing forward so that it can be identified immediately when entering the storage area. You can

also label the wall, floor, or shelf area where the item is located so that you can return it to the correct location when you're finished using it. Using clear containers when possible is a great way to easily assess what is inside, too.

- **Evaluate the practical usage of seasonal items.** If you haven't used objects, such as decor and sports equipment, within the past year, eliminate them. One year is a good rule of thumb because within that time all occasions and seasons have passed once.
- **Arrange items by frequency of use.** Place frequently used items toward the front of the area or in an easily accessible location within reach and eyesight. Place seasonal and less frequently used items toward the back of the space or higher up on shelves. Place large items in corners and away from entrances and exits.
- **Utilize wall and ceiling space for storage.** Save floor and shelf space by hanging items on the wall or ceiling. Hanging can be ideal for sports equipment, tools, and corded items.

The home can be one of the most challenging areas to simplify, but with these strategies you're more than prepared to develop a home space that you love and that supports your priorities. In this chapter, we evaluated the clutter in your home and provided tips for eliminating it, in addition to ways to organize and make spaces more visually appealing. In chapter 4, we'll look at the second most used space in many of our lives: the office.

Chapter 4

Office and Work Space

After our homes, we spend most of our time at work. Ideally, we want to create a working environment that is representative of both our lifestyle and career goals. We face a similar clutter issue at work as we do in our homes with paper and documents, but the workplace presents its own challenges because we may be subject to policies and space constraints beyond our control. Still, there are strategies we can employ to make our offices more conducive to focusing on being productive and meeting our objectives.

Strategies for Simplifying
Your Work Space

Let's pause and reflect on the top three priorities you set for the work space in chapter 2. Feel free to jot down notes about your priorities on the lines below. When working through the tips for simplifying your work space, keep your *why* and your values in mind as you consider how these tips can help you meet those priorities. Remember the benefits of staying present during this process.

_____

_____

_____

Addressing Clutter in Your Work Space

Whether you have your own office or cubicle or you share a work space with others, it's necessary to assess the physical space. If you share a work space, you should conduct this evaluation with your coworkers. Physical clutter can affect your creativity, productivity, and morale. Organizing and simplifying your work area will create the space for you to implement all other strategies to decrease your mental clutter.

- **Evaluate your desk supplies.** Determine how frequently you use those supplies. Keep the essentials visible on your desk in an easily accessible location. Place a few backups of those frequently used supplies in a drawer and return any excess or unused supplies to the supply closet.

- **Limit company paraphernalia.** If your job requires you to interact with the public or with clients, you may need to be more mindful about how you display company-branded items, but you can still limit them to one or two pieces. If you don't interact with customers, feel free to only keep and display a company item that you really love or that has meaning and remove the rest.

- **Clean out old food and drink items from the breakroom.** Doing this weekly will ensure nothing spoils or is taking up needed space in the refrigerator and cabinets. Bringing snacks and beverages from home that help you focus or give you energy is a great idea, but be mindful of their usage and storage.

- **Clean out your work bag.** Remove trash and anything not related to work. Also, remove papers not associated with the current projects you're working on. If you have an ID badge for work, place it in an area or secure pocket that is easily reachable.
- **Tidy and organize your workspace at the end of each day.** This will prevent clutter from building up. When you return to work, your space will be clear and ready for business.
- **Rearrange your office.** Switching the layout of your desk and other furniture could have a great effect on your performance. Consider the ideal physical conditions you need in order to be productive. Also, account for your personal items in your workspace. Go through your photos and trinkets and choose only a few items to display that keep you connected to your life outside of work.

Being Efficient and Productive

Productivity is a measure of your performance. Beyond the importance of how much work you complete, you should also consider the quality of that work. Efficiency is one of the characteristics that all managers look for in skilled workers. The following strategies can assist you in producing high-quality work with less stress.

- **Make short to-do lists.** Try limiting your daily to-dos to three or four essential items based on your priorities and your team's current priorities and goals. Set a goal of accomplishing one or two items before your main break and one or two more afterward. Take a few minutes every day to select the most important tasks you must complete. Having a long agenda does not make you more productive and can be demoralizing when you don't accomplish it all. Shorter lists increase the likelihood you'll complete everything within the day and eventually finish the longer list you had within the week. Write your list for the next day before you leave work and make it visible on your desk. Writing your list the night before ensures that you will not waste any time starting work when you arrive the next day.

- **Block your time.** Take a moment to sketch out your usual work day from arrival to departure. Think about the times when you tend to be most productive and create 2-hour blocks, using a timer if necessary and buffered by short breaks of up to 30 minutes. Focus on one or two tasks during those hours per the previous strategy. If that's not how you work, work on as much as you can during that period but stop working when the time is up. Do not work on your break. Go take a walk, have a snack, or do something to clear your mind until you return for your next time block.

- **Break down large objectives into smaller tasks.** Similar to long to-do lists, duties associated with large projects can seem daunting. Review your personal responsibilities and break those down into smaller assignments that you can spread out over time until the due date. You can also create your own personal deadlines for these tasks ahead of the main deadline.

- **Decrease the number of meetings you attend.** This may require a conversation with your supervisor or team. A study conducted by Bain & Company in collaboration with 17 large companies found that organizations use 15 percent of company time for meetings, and if you work in a management or supervisory role, this number is greater. While 15 percent may not seem like much, if we think about a standard 40-hour workweek, that is six hours spent in meetings, almost a full workday. Not all meetings are avoidable, but if your role is nonessential, ask to be excused. If it's a larger department meeting, perhaps designate someone on your team to attend the meeting and report back. Team members can take turns doing this.

- **Flex your time and use your paid time off.** Review your company's policies on alternative work schedules, flextime, and using paid time off. If you're working additional hours or feel that working from home some days could be beneficial, ask if your schedule can be altered temporarily or permanently to balance your total time worked with your lifestyle needs. Finally, use your paid time off! In 2017, the US Travel Association reported 52 percent of Americans had unused paid time off at the end of the year. It doesn't matter if you're taking a staycation or the occasional mental health day, it's important to be away from work beyond your normal days off. Taking additional time off helps you clear the mental clutter accumulated from work and return refreshed.

Organizing Papers and Files

Paper is one of the more insidious forms of clutter in a work setting, even as workplaces move toward digitized documentation and computerized processes. We still use a lot of paper that ends up in piles on our desks and fills up our drawers. It's even common for people to print out communications, such as e-mails and other information obtained electronically. Decreasing the amount of paper in your work space can go a long way to reducing overall clutter.

- **Archive old files per your company's standards.** If there are boxes of old files or a file cabinet not being used, request to have maintenance remove them from your office or work area. As soon as a project is complete or a client relationship ends, archive the files associated with it.

- **Digitize and scan files as soon as possible.** Your company likely uses electronic document viewing software such as Adobe Acrobat, so utilize it to scan documents and do away with the paper files. Digital files are also very useful if you tend to work from home or travel frequently for work.

- **Use your office's shredder to eliminate nonessential paperwork.** Destroy files that have been scanned, as well as duplicate and triplicate copies. If your office does not own a shredder, make sure all unwanted paperwork is torn up and recycled.

- **Create a physical inbox and outbox.** For paper documents you must keep, establish a physical space to organize them on your desk. Similar to your home mail organization, this ensures important items are marked, visible, and less likely to be overlooked.

- **Establish a monthly routine to review files.** Paperwork usually must be archived, digitized, shredded, or recycled. Determine a schedule to sort through your files to avoid unnecessary clutter. This routine may take place at the end of the month but should logically follow your personal work cycles or the company's business cycles.

Organizing Your Electronic Files

Your technological devices are your key to staying organized. Once you have simplified your paper clutter, the next step is to address your electronic calendar, desktop, e-mail, and documents. Electronic organization is a powerful resource because it allows you to store a higher volume and variety of items in one place.

- **Sync your devices.** If you use multiple devices for work—such as a desktop computer, laptop, and mobile phone—connect all devices to each other so that they update at the same time. Syncing your devices' calendars, applications, and files keeps you on track when you're away from your desk or the office. It will also enable you to add notes and reminders to follow up on when you return to the office. Additionally, if you use a physical calendar or agenda, ensure it is properly updated.

- **Schedule all tasks, meetings, breaks, and time off on your calendar.** Electronic calendars can usually color-code different types of events, set reminders, block off periods of time, and share your calendar with others. It is a good accountability practice to share appropriate work information from your calendar with your supervisor and team. They will know what you're working on, when to expect certain objectives to be completed, and when you're not going to be present. They will also be notified when changes are made so that everyone can plan accordingly. This can simplify your workday by keeping everyone on the same page.
- **Declutter and organize desktop icons.** Only keep software and application icons that you use daily on your computer's desktop and remove all others. Similarly, keep folder icons with documents you access frequently on your desktop. Choose an organization system that makes sense to you, such as alphabetization, categorization, or ranking.
- **Declutter and organize electronic files and documents.** As with paper files, you will need to check your company's policies for archiving and deleting documents. Once you've sifted through them all, use folders to organize them with a system. It may make sense to

arrange them by project, policy, client, or date. Empty your digital trash can periodically. Remember that every program, document, image, folder, and icon uses space and memory on your device.

- **Declutter and organize e-mails.** In 2015, the Radicati Group noted in their *Email Statistics Report* that business-people sent and received an average of 122 e-mails per day. Even if you aren't dealing with hundreds of e-mails per day, you're likely receiving dozens and that could pile up over time if you're not regularly deleting and filing them. While sorting through your e-mails, choose an organization system to manage them and use the priority settings to denote important contacts and e-mails you don't want to miss.

Assessing Your Job

Just as you have assessed the physical environment of your work space, you should also evaluate the mental commitments of your job. This can be especially useful if you have been working in your career for more than several years. If you have been in your position for less than a year, it's important that you are clear about what is expected of you and what you can deliver.

- **Review your official job description.** Compare it to your actual duties and responsibilities. Look for areas where you want to increase your responsibilities or experience, as well as duties that could be eliminated or delegated to other team members.

- **Find the intersections between your department's priorities and your own.** Determine if the work you're doing is in alignment with your company's stated objectives and your personal work goals. Happiness and satisfaction can be found where they overlap. Try using a Venn diagram (overlapping circles) to find the differences and similarities.

- **Schedule a check-in with your supervisor.** This is especially helpful if you have not had a one-on-one meeting in the past three to six months. Find out how you are doing, what you are doing well, and what could be improved. If you have concerns about your performance or role on the team, now is the time to address them. This is good practice for approaching situations proactively and it strengthens the relationship between you and your superior.

- **Set boundaries regarding after-hours communication and work.** Use out-of-office messages, let your team know you will not respond to messages after a certain time or on your off-days, and, if possible, turn off your work phone and other devices at the end of the workday. If you receive communication on your personal phone, turn off notifications and utilize the "do not disturb" setting.

Taking the steps outlined in this chapter is crucial because your work is a significant contributor to your quality of life. Not only did we identify strategies for decluttering your physical work environment, but we also addressed how to increase your productivity and job satisfaction to reduce mental clutter. Next, we'll examine another area that greatly impacts our lifestyle: family life.

Chapter 5

——

Family Life

Family life is closely entangled with the home. Having a simple family life involves finding routines that work for your family and committing to them. Simplifying your family life creates space for strong familial connections.

Strategies for Simplifying Your Family Life

Let's pause and reflect on the top three priorities you set for your family life in chapter 2. Feel free to jot down notes about your priorities on the lines below. Allow these priorities to guide you as you think through these strategies to streamline your family's time, responsibilities, and possessions. Additionally, keep your *why* and your values in mind as you consider how these tips can help you meet those priorities. Don't forget to remain present as you apply these strategies.

_____

_____

_____

Addressing Your Family's Schedule

Work, school, extracurricular activities, household responsibilities, appointments, errands, and special events all require successful management. Keeping up with everyone's calendar can be challenging and cause undue stress and mental clutter. Now is the perfect time to evaluate what everyone is doing, determine if it is working for your family, and use the following strategies to keep everyone in your family on track.

- **Use a physical calendar and a digital calendar.** The physical calendar should be displayed in your home in a common family area, such as the kitchen or living room. The digital calendar should match the physical calendar and be synced to all family members' devices. The calendar should have everyone's activities and chores listed. This will ensure everyone is aware of their own responsibilities and nothing is forgotten in the hustle and bustle of daily life.

- **Practice independence and cooperation.** Each family member is responsible for cleaning and maintaining personal items and spaces. For shared spaces—such as the kitchen, living room, and bathrooms—work out a plan to share the responsibility, either by cleaning together or rotating the chore.

- **Batch chores.** After reviewing the family calendar, choose a couple of times each week where everyone has free time to do chores together. Put on some energetic music and make it a family affair.

- **Schedule family time.** It can be easy for family members to get caught up in their own worlds, so it's possible that families aren't spending as much quality time together as they think. Make it a point to schedule family time weekly or monthly to discuss family issues and to just spend time together and have fun.

- **Eliminate unnecessary commitments.** If there are activities you (or your family members) are involved in that aren't beneficial to your mental or physical health, do not meet your top priorities, or you absolutely dislike, cancel them. Your only responsibility as a family is to honor the priorities you set for your household.

Managing Clothing and Laundry

Clothing is another item that can accumulate uncontrollably, and it's one of the top sources of frustration that people want to simplify. Shopping, cleaning, and storing our clothes costs us money, energy, and time. The following tips will help you reduce the amount of clothing you own and cut down on laundry time.

- **Declutter your clothing.** Dispose of anything you haven't worn in six months to one year, doesn't fit, is faded, is damaged beyond reasonable repair, or is not your personal style. Create four piles: keep, toss, donate, and unsure. You have two options to manage the unsure pile: 1) Toss the clothes, because you don't have a strong feeling about them positively or negatively. 2) Place the items you're unsure of in the front of your wardrobe to see if you choose those pieces when getting dressed. Only donate clothing that is in good condition and toss whatever is unfit to donate.

- **Pick a personal uniform.** The easiest way to simplify your clothing is to wear the same thing often. Pay attention to what clothing items you wear the most and eliminate the rest. With a uniform, you don't have to waste time thinking about what to wear, and it can save you money by shopping less frequently for the latest trends. If you're not interested in a uniform, consider picking a color scheme and applying it to your wardrobe. Getting dressed is simple when everything matches.

- **Separate laundry bins and wash times.** Let all family members have their own laundry baskets and teach them how to sort their clothing as it becomes dirty. Wash the children's clothing separate from the adults', and if the children are old enough, allow them to do their own laundry. Adults can do their own laundry, too, so that no one is overburdened with the task.

- **Wash fewer loads at off-peak times.** Washing fewer loads at one time may reduce some of the drudgery of doing laundry. If you're following the previous tip and sorting your laundry as you go, once a basket of one type of laundry is full, go ahead and wash it instead of waiting for multiple loads to pile up, requiring more hours to wash. Washing in the mornings and evenings tends to save on energy costs, but verify off-peak times with your power company.

- **Hang clothing instead of folding.** Some clothing such as intimates and nightclothes may be better folded, but most other clothing can be hung. Hanging is quicker than folding and, if you hang your clothing as soon as it comes out of the dryer, you can reduce wrinkling so you won't need to iron as often.

Tidying Toys

As children grow, it is easy for toys to become clutter. Children receive toys for holidays, birthdays, and other occasions from their parents, relatives, and family friends. Toys are useful to engage children's minds, teach valuable skills and knowledge, and keep them occupied, but they should not be excessive. Children are naturally creative and, with fewer toys, they will have more opportunities to explore their limitless imaginations.

- **Declutter the toys.** With your children, look at each item and determine if they still play with it and if it is age-appropriate. Remove any toys that are broken, missing pieces, unused, or that your kid has outgrown. If your children are having trouble letting go of their toys, ask them to choose toys they want to gift a less fortunate child. Toys, games, and sometimes clothing are especially wanted at family and domestic abuse shelters. Churches and charity organizations may also accept toy donations.

- **Follow the one-in/one-out rule.** Every time your children get a new toy, release at least one old one. If your children are asking for a large or expensive birthday or Christmas gift, ask them to give up several items in exchange. In general, decluttering toys and games may be easier to do right before gift-giving holidays. Keep in mind that the one-in/one-out rule can work in many other situations to manage belongings.

- **Ask for alternative gifts.** Notify relatives and friends ahead of holidays and birthdays that your children don't need any more toys. Possible gift alternatives include gift cards, experiences, and donations to a scholarship account or charity.

- **Limit the number of toys your children can have.** There is no magical number that is enough because every child has different needs, but you can certainly aim to reduce their current stash by at least half. Evaluate the educational and creative value of each toy you choose to keep. When you exceed the maximum number, decide what can be removed.

- **Designate a space in your children's bedroom for their toys.** This area should fit all of the toys and games they own and be easily accessible. Place smaller toys in containers that are child-friendly, too.

- **Check to see if your city has a toy library.** Public libraries may also lend toys, games, and learning kits. This could save you a lot of money and give your children a greater variety of toys to experience. Borrowing toys from a library can also teach your children about sharing and letting go.

Structuring Bedtime

Evenings can be a difficult time to simplify. We are tired from work, school, or errands and it takes most of the energy we have left to have the kids do their homework, fix something for dinner, relax for a little while, and then go to bed at a reasonable time. Creating a routine that works for you and your family will help bedtime go smoothly so that you can get a good night's rest and be mentally and physically prepared for the next day.

- **Set an actual bedtime and program it into your phone.** Set one bedtime for yourself and one for your children and stick to it every day. This time should provide enough space for you to complete your routine, have some relaxation time, and get enough hours of sleep before you have to wake up the next day. Once you've determined the ideal bedtime, set an alarm for 30 minutes before this time and another one for the actual time. Use the 30 minutes to wind down by turning off all screens and devices, putting your pajamas on, and getting comfortable in your bed.
- **Turn off all devices while you sleep.** If you need your phone turned on for an alarm, utilize the "do not disturb" feature. Don't worry about missing an emergency call or message because you can edit the "do not disturb" settings to allow communication from contacts you select. This ensures your sleep will not be interrupted unnecessarily during the night by unwanted calls.

- **Create a comfortable sleeping environment.** According to the National Sleep Foundation, the best environment for sleep is a cool, dark, and quiet room. Remove distractions such as work items and turn off your televisions and any screens that emit light. The Foundation also suggests avoiding caffeine, alcohol, and spicy food a few hours before bedtime.
- **Establish your "before bedtime" routine.** Take baths and showers, pick out your clothing, and prepare breakfast and lunch for the next day. Remember to include relaxing activities before bedtime such as reading or listening to a book, working on puzzles, or practicing a mindful activity such as meditation or prayer. A routine prepares the mind and body for sleep and clears mental clutter.

Building Family Support

Building and maintaining strong family connections is the key to a harmonious family life. It is the foundation upon which you can make needed and lasting changes that will solidify your family unit. It can improve communication, simplify challenges, and help all members build and strengthen social skills. Some of these strategies may be challenging because they require mental and emotional energy to practice. However, once established, your family will be grateful for the bond that exists, and it will make life easier to experience together.

- **Establish your family values and rules.** Schedule a specific meeting just to talk about what's most important to the family unit. Individuals can share their personal values, and together you can find commonalities. Values can be recommended, discussed, and then chosen as a family. These values can be added to the family calendar so they are always visible. Similarly, set some time aside to determine the family rules. What ground rules should your family follow for the home to run smoothly? Your rules can include guidelines about responsibilities, privacy, scheduling, making requests, and anything you deem necessary.

- **Schedule one-on-one time.** A family is a group composed of individuals. Among those individuals, there are separate relationships that exist within the family. It's important that partners have alone time with each other, that each parent has one-on-one time with each child, and that siblings spend time together. Allow space for these individual relationships to exist and develop. Guidelines for spending one-on-one time with each other can be included in the family rules.

- **Respect each other's individual values, interests, privacy, and alone time.** Again, recognizing that a family is made up of unique personalities, we should nurture and respect each person's uniqueness. When all family members feel free to be themselves and feel supported, family bonds are fortified and each person contributes to the family unit from a position of empowerment. Details regarding the ways to respect one another can be included in the family rules.

- **Offer gratitude, praise, and affection.** Acknowledgment is a powerful tool for building and maintaining support and rapport within the family. The people you love need and want to know what they mean to you. Acknowledgment also promotes an atmosphere of positivity. Make it a habit of thanking your family members not only when they help you, but also for simply being in your life. Uplift them when they accomplish something that is meaningful to them, big or small. Showing verbal and physical affection makes your family feel cherished, and it teaches your children how to love and treat others.

- **Identify the helpers.** There are times when you'll need assistance from people outside your family. In the event you cannot provide the support they need, such as with an illness or emergency, it is critical your family members know who they can contact for help. Make them aware of relatives, friends, neighbors, coworkers, and other folks they can rely on in times of need. It's also a good idea to let those helpers know they have been designated as such, so that they're not caught off-guard if they receive a call.
- **Schedule family leisure time.** Every family needs time to cut loose and take a break from the normal routines and expectations. This time is just as important as family meetings where you discuss values, rules, and family issues. Family fun time can be as simple as a game night, movie night, or backyard barbeque. Planning a staycation in your city is also an easy way to explore what your city has to offer without traveling too far or spending a lot of money. If you're planning a more involved vacation, allow plenty of time to research options, set a budget to plan within, and allow everyone to have input on the experience.

In this chapter, we examined the ways family life is connected to the home, as well as how your family members use their time and how they relate to each other. We also discussed the need to focus more closely on the habits and routines of your family's daily life. We covered simplifying physical items, such as clothing and toys, but more importantly, we reviewed strategies for how to strengthen family bonds and maximize family time. Money is an important factor in how a household is managed and we'll assess that next.

Chapter 6

———

Finances and Budgeting

Money is a topic that makes some people uncomfortable; however, it is another aspect of simple living that you must address. Thinking about your finances can be stressful if you haven't learned valuable strategies and tools to manage your money successfully. This chapter will provide the tips you need to plan, make informed economic decisions, and spend your money mindfully.

Strategies for Simplifying Your Finances

It's time to review the three priorities you chose for your finances in chapter 2. If it's helpful, write a few notes about those priorities on the lines below and keep in mind your *why* and your values as you read through these tips. Recall the importance of staying present during this process.

_____

_____

_____

Addressing Your Money Habits

Now is the time to get clear about how you've been handling your money up to this point. If you've made mistakes in the past, it's okay. You have an opportunity to be honest with yourself and face the results of your money mind-set. The following strategies will help you evaluate the current state of your finances by allowing you to understand your expenses, income sources, open accounts, and credit history. These practices will prepare you to address the other strategies in this chapter.

- **Track your expenses.** Where is your money going? Spend some time reviewing all your transactions from the past 30 days. View your purchases from the past month to help you get an overview of where your money is going regularly. If you'd like a fuller picture, you can look at your transactions from the past quarter. How much did you spend on fixed expenses, such as your mortgage or rent, insurance, and car? What were your variable costs for items like utilities and food during the month? Finally, how much did you spend on discretionary or unnecessary items, like entertainment? Consider if you can meet your financial priorities with your current spending habits.

- **Understand your income.** For many people, their sole source of income is from their full-time job, but you may also receive income from a part-time job, an inheritance, a settlement, or government benefits such as social security. Calculate the total income you receive monthly and compare it to the amount you spend each month. Does your income exceed, break even with, or fall below your expenses? The difference between your income and expenses will give you clues about where to simplify.

- **Collect all your financial statements.** To get a complete picture of your finances, you need to look at all of your accounts. Gather the most recent copies of your mortgage, car loan, student loans, and any other account statements. Also find your bank, credit card, insurance, and any investment statements you may have, as well as last year's tax return. Simply looking at your bank transactions will not show the entire picture. Statements show the total amounts due or remaining, how much you've paid, and accumulated interest and fees. This will be important later in this chapter. This is also a good time to see if any charges can be eliminated in the future.

- **Pull your credit report.** Do you look at your credit report regularly? It is recommended to check it at least annually. Some people do not look at them until they need to apply for credit or if there is a problem. By that time, it may be too late to catch inaccuracies or fraudulent activity before you're denied credit or service. Bill payments, loans, the number and history of accounts, legal judgments, and more can impact your credit score. In turn, your credit score determines if you're financially worthy to do basic things such as rent or buy a house or car. Some companies check potential employees' credit reports before hiring them. Knowing your score and working to raise it can improve your financial health. You can get a free copy of your credit report at AnnualCreditReport.com, and there are free services such as Credit Karma and Credit Sesame that provide credit history information. Your bank may also offer a complimentary credit report.

- **Analyze your money mind-set.** Think about how you learned what you know about money. Did you learn from your parents or guardians, either by them teaching you or by watching them? Did you learn on your own when you became an adult? What is your relationship with money? Do you operate from a place of abundance or scarcity? Take a few moments to think about or write your answers to those questions. Just as you want healthy relationships with yourself and others, you want a healthy monetary relationship. Decide right now how you want to relate to your money going forward.

Creating and Maintaining a Budget

No matter how much or how little money you have, everyone needs a budget. A budget is a plan for your money. Your budget tells your money what to do and helps you stay on track with your goals and financial obligations. Having a budget gives you control over your money and can help you see where you need to make improvements. With a budget, there are no doubts about where your money is going. These strategies will help you build a budget, personalize it, and stick with it.

- **Create a simple budget.** You're already halfway there. In the previous section, I had you list all of your expenses and your income. This is basically what a budget is: an accounting of your expenses and income. Get a piece of paper or open a spreadsheet on your computer. Take the list of your expenses and prioritize them. I put my most important expenses—such as rent, food, and transportation—at the top. If you want to further organize your budget, you can categorize your expenses by type—such as housing, transportation, utilities, and insurance—and then list the individual expenses accordingly. You can also budget savings for emergencies, vacations, special items, and retirement. Depending on what works for you, you can structure your budget monthly, quarterly, or annually.

- **Follow and review your budget on schedule.** As you pay your bills, cross-check the transactions and balance of your bank account with your budget. If you're tracking your budget, make notations as items are completed. If your income is variable from paycheck to paycheck or received monthly, make sure to update your budget to reflect that. Decide how often you will review your budget. Reevaluate and update your budget periodically, such as monthly or quarterly, and after any major life changes.

- **Experiment with different types of budgets.** Once you've mastered the simple budget, you can try others that meet your specific needs. You could try a zero-based budget, which takes into account every cent of your income. You can design a budget around a specific goal you have, such as being debt-free, planning for a special event like a wedding or vacation, or retirement. If you have a part-time job or business, you may need to create multiple budgets.

- **Budget together.** If you live with others, like a partner or children, make budgeting a family affair. You will not be solely responsible for managing the household's finances, and you can teach your children valuable skills about managing money. Even if you live alone, you can consult a financial advisor for suggestions on creating and maintaining a successful budget. Your bank, local government, or library may offer free financial planning services.

- **Stick to your budget.** Your budget only works if you don't deviate from it. To see changes, you will need to budget consistently. Things come up and emergencies happen, but you will be better prepared to respond to unplanned expenses if you're budgeting routinely. Take a mobile picture of your paper budget so that you have it with you at all times or sync your electronic budget across devices. Program reminders into your calendar for payment due dates and periodic budget reviews.

Managing Credit and Debt

Credit and debt are inextricably linked. Your credit-worthiness is determined by your credit history and score. It can give you an indication of how much debt you can take on, assuming you also have stable and sufficient income. To learn how to access your credit report, refer back to the "Addressing Your Money Habits" section. CNBC reported the average American had $38,000 of personal debt in 2018. If you own a house, went to college, or had a prolonged illness or medical emergency at some point, it's likely you have debt. It's also likely you have at least one credit card. These are the most common types of debt we carry. You can reduce and eliminate your debt if that is one of your financial priorities.

- **Know how much you owe.** Reference your loan statements again. Make sure you have information from all sources of your debt. What is the total amount you owe? This figure should include the principle balances, as well as interest and fees that have been added. Review the terms of your debt payback and be clear about those terms. When are the expected payment dates based on your current terms? If you don't understand all the terms or have questions about what is owed and past payments, make time to contact the debt servicer.

- **Refinance or consolidate loans.** You may need to consult with a financial advisor before attempting this, but renegotiating the terms of your loans could save you money. If you have many different debt servicers, inquire about consolidating as many of your debts as possible with one financial company. This will make it easier to keep track of your debts.

- **Make a plan to pay off debt.** Debt freedom is a priority for many people. Paying off your debt sooner can save you money over the course of your loan; improve your credit eligibility, including access to lower interest rates; and help you achieve financial security. Money not paid toward loan interest is more money that can be put toward savings and investments. There are many options for attacking your debt. A popular one is the snowball method, by which you start paying more toward the smallest debt and work your way up to the larger ones. It's popular because it's easier to pay off smaller debts more quickly, and seeing those fast results gives you the encouragement to keep going. You could also pay the largest debt first, pay down based on the interest rate, or choose another method that works for you. The key is to have a plan and stick with it. You'll also want to consider ways you can bring in more money to help pay your debts off quickly. For example, you can sell some of your things (and declutter at the same time) or take on odd jobs.
- **Limit credit cards and pay more than the minimum.** Credit card companies specialize in marketing a variety of deals to customers to entice you to apply, and once you get one, it's generally easier to get others.

You may use several cards for different purposes, but it's best to simplify to one or two cards, or none if you don't feel they are benefitting your financial health. With multiple cards, you can lose track of purchases and due dates and instead of focusing on managing and paying off one card responsibly, you may shift unnecessary purchases around to other cards, increasing your overall balance. With credit cards and any other debt, whenever possible, pay more than the minimum payment. Minimum payments are usually applied incrementally to your principal and interest. Paying above the minimum applies more money to the principle and reduces interest. You can also contact your loan servicer and ask them how your payments are being applied. You might be able to change the way it's applied to get more bang for your buck.

- **Go cash only.** You can limit your usage of credit and reduce debt accrual overall by using cash more frequently. Buy only what your money can afford. This may mean renting a house instead of buying one, getting a nice used car instead of financing a new one, only taking cash when going out shopping, laying away items that require you to pay in full before you can pick them up, and using a prepaid card you load with cash instead of a credit card to make purchases. Keep track of cash purchases by requesting and saving receipts for each transaction. For purchases where no receipt is available, keep a running list in your phone or notebook.

Building Your Savings

Although mindfulness focuses on being in the moment, being financially prepared for the future can ease your mind in the present. Your savings should be multifaceted to address your future plans, which should account for the needs and wants you will encounter as you age. If you have a partner or family, your savings plan should also include them.

- **Create an emergency fund.** To determine the amount of money you need in your emergency fund, you should multiply your monthly expenses by as many months as you feel you can comfortably survive on your savings. A good range is at least three to six months of emergency savings. This will give you time to explore new job opportunities and streams of income, if necessary. Also consider unplanned expenses, such as car and home repairs. It may take time for you to reach this desired amount, but don't be discouraged by how much money you are starting with. Just put something into a savings account to get started.

- **Invest in your retirement.** You can establish a retirement fund through your job (if they offer those benefits) or you can create your own with a financial institution of your choice. Planning for retirement requires you to realistically think about the quality of life you expect to have in your golden years and what you can comfortably live off of (it's likely to be less than your current income). You must also anticipate changes in your household, health, and other areas. This can be complex, so it's a good idea to consult with an advisor. Your company may have representatives or you can talk to someone at your local financial institution, in addition to doing your own research. Contribute the maximum annual amount to your retirement account, if possible, and take advantage of any available company match programs through which your company will contribute a percentage of your investment each year.

- **Plan how you will pay for higher education.** Americans owe approximately $1.5 trillion in student loan debt, and the average borrower from the Class of 2017 holds about $29,000 in debt, as reported in

Forbes. If you have children who want to go to college or you plan to attend or return to college in the future, you should start saving immediately. College costs have increased considerably over the past several decades and are likely to continue as we face the student loan debt crisis. Determine what you can save after funding your emergency and retirement savings. Check with your state government and bank about college savings plans.

- **Check for "found" money.** Don't leave any money lying around when thinking about your financial future. Most local and state governments have sites where you can check to see if you have any unclaimed monies and property. This could be inheritances, tax overpayments, or settlements. You're not guaranteed to find anything, but it takes only a few minutes to be sure. If you have elderly or deceased parents, it's a good idea to check their names and addresses in the database too.

- **Estimate tax payments and plan for potential refunds.** Speaking of taxes, if you know you will owe money next year, you can start saving now. If you're anticipating a refund, make a plan for what you will do with it. It could be put toward a retirement or emergency fund or used to pay off debt.

Using Tools to Manage Your Finances

Knowing what tools are available and using them habitually will reduce much of the discomfort associated with managing your finances and make it easier to maintain strong money habits. The right technology, combined with willpower and a focus on your priorities, will help you mindfully master your funds.

- **Automate everything.** Bill payments can be automatically withdrawn and transferred as they're due. Automation can be scheduled through your bank account or directly with the company you're paying. Cross-check your due dates with your scheduled pay dates to ensure you don't overspend on your account. Check with your bank about overdraft protection and linking your savings to your checking to prevent overdrafts. You can also schedule regular transfers from your checking to your savings account.

- **Review your insurance protection.** We hope it's never needed, but it's best to be prepared. A serious illness, accident, or death can derail your financial plans and even lead to bankruptcy. We typically need several types of insurance, including life, health, and property insurance. Other types of insurance such as accident, disability, and long-term care may be a smart choice for you and your family. Check your amount of coverage for each item and your premiums. Also review the terms of your insurance agreements so that you're aware of the conditions.

- **Digitize your records.** This includes contracts, warranties, a copy of your budget, and your will, among others. You will need to keep paper copies of some financial records, so make sure to keep them in one secure place. For the ones where a paper copy is not required, destroy and recycle them after you digitize them. You can also scan and keep an image of your important receipts in your phone, computer, or cloud storage.

- **Use smartphone applications.** Most banks now have mobile banking apps. Use them to track purchases and deposits and make transfers on the go. There are apps to create and manage your budget, to save and invest, and to send and receive money from others.

With the strategies presented in this chapter, you've learned tips for how to evaluate your current money habits, create and keep a budget, and tackle and decrease your debt. We've also covered what kinds of savings you need and the tools to solidify and maintain good financial habits. Our relationship to money has a huge impact on our quality of life as Americans living in a capitalist economy. Mastering your money will produce positive shifts in other areas of your life such as your home, family life, and shopping habits. What we buy is directly related to our financial habits and mind-set, which we'll address next.

Chapter 7

—

Shopping

As much as we want to reduce our spending, we cannot avoid shopping completely because we have to purchase essentials like food, household items, and clothing. While shopping, we're likely to allow our emotions to influence our consumption behavior, overspend, and throw our budgets off track.

Strategies for Simplifying Shopping

Pause to remind yourself of the top three priorities you chose for shopping. Feel free to make notes about those priorities on the lines below. Keep your *why* and your values in mind as you consider these priorities. Remember to remain present as you apply the following strategies to simplify your shopping habits.

_____

_____

_____

Addressing Your Consumption Habits

Before we begin streamlining your consumption habits, we should look at the patterns you've developed thus far. Let's address the popular notion of retail therapy and how it serves neither ourselves nor our visions for a simplified life. Being aware of how and why you shop and your challenges while shopping will help you curb this behavior in the future and make sensible purchases.

- **Ditch retail therapy.** Detach yourself from the idea that buying things will solve your personal issues. While it may be true that buying things makes us feel better temporarily, retail therapy is a form of escapism, which we learned in chapter 1 is one of the five compensatory behaviors we tend to engage in when consuming things. When the high of the purchase wears off, you're still left with the problem and unresolved emotions. When you feel off-balance or uncomfortable, be brave and sit with those feelings. Use what you have learned about mindfulness to address how you feel and find a healthy solution.

- **Analyze how often you shop.** Do you make several trips per week or a couple of shopping trips per month? Frequent shoppers should consider making fewer trips to decrease spending. Making fewer trips can encourage mindfulness about what you're purchasing and your rate of consumption. Are there certain times of the month when you shop more than others? Look at the dates of your purchases to find patterns so that you can break them.

- **Determine how much you spend.** Take a moment and look at your figures from the "Addressing Your Money Habits" section in chapter 6. In the past month, what did you spend on purchases? How many receipts did you accumulate from shopping? Now, looking at those figures, how much money did you spend on absolute necessities, such as groceries and household basics, and how much did you spend on luxuries, such as eating out or going to the movies? Aside from your necessities, is there one area where you spend more than the others? Keep these numbers in mind as you think about your priorities.

- **Figure out what type of shopper you are.** There are several types of shopper personalities and knowing which one you are can assist you in shopping mindfully. Personal finance expert Dave Ramsey identified some of the most common profiles: The Bargain Hunter, The Impulse Buyer, The Researcher, and The Brand Loyalist. Do you want the cheapest deal? Do you allow your emotions to make your decisions? Do you compare prices and features? Or do you stick with the company you've known forever, regardless of the price? It's possible you fit more than one of these profiles, such as being a bargain hunter and researcher (that's me!), but the important thing is to know what motivates you when shopping. When you identify the type of shopper you are, you can unpack why you resort to this spending behavior.

- **Consider if you shop online or in stores.** Besides knowing the type of shopper you are, you should also be mindful of where you do the bulk of your shopping. If you're an online shopper, you may want to take precautions, such as deleting store apps from your phone and limiting online browsing time, to reduce spending. If you're a traditional in-store shopper, avoiding malls, outlets, and shopping centers can help keep purchases in check.

Minimizing Clothing

Clothing can be a challenge because it is both a necessity and a desire. We need clothing for our daily activities and we want to look stylish, or at least decent, in the process. While it's fine to want to portray an image we feel is consistent with our personality, problems arise when acquiring the clothing becomes more important than developing ourselves. We may get caught up in sales and comparing ourselves to others and we may believe buying the clothes will magically enhance our personalities. Clothing alone is not that powerful, and it ends up piling up in our closets and laundry baskets as we convince ourselves we have nothing to wear and perpetuate the cycle of consumption. The strategies below will help you build an intentional wardrobe, save money, and break the cycle.

- **Swap your clothing.** Similar to the home decor swap, this strategy can be employed with clothing as well. You could advertise the swap as a neighborhood event to draw more people or choose to swap with your close friends and relatives. Ask them to bring unwanted clothing and accessories in good condition. You can get a whole new wardrobe for free! Once the swap is over, designate one or two people to toss or donate the unwanted clothes.

- **Borrow or rent clothes.** Do you have a special occasion coming up, but you don't want to go shopping or don't have the time? Save yourself both time and money by borrowing an outfit from someone you know who is a similar size with a comparable style. There are also companies that rent clothing and formal wear, such as Rent the Runway, an online business that allows you to wear the latest designer fashions for a fee. Don't waste money purchasing something at full price you're likely to wear only once or twice.

- **Go thrifting.** You can find unique and inexpensive clothing in thrift stores and consignment shops. Go thrifting with an idea in mind, so that you don't end up mindlessly buying all the little trinkets. Thrifting is an example of slow fashion. The clothing is being recycled, extending its life cycle, and it can take time to find the pieces you are looking for. The benefit of wearing slow fashion is that it allows you the time and space to be intentional about your wardrobe and style. If you don't like thrifting, there are many shops on eBay, Etsy, and Instagram that curate items based on a particular style, which can make it simpler for you to find those unique pieces for your wardrobe without the hassle of going from store to store.

- **Shop at the end of the season or off-season.** When you want or need to buy new clothing, it's best to wait for off-peak times when the current or previous season's items will be heavily discounted. The new season's clothing may be on sale at the end of the current season as a preview. Traditional retail stores are typically trying to get rid of the last season's clothing to make space for new items and may have mark-downs in addition to clearance prices. This is generally true for online stores as well.

Shopping for Food

Comparable to clothing, food shopping is another area where we tend to overconsume because food fulfills our physical and emotional needs. Our bodies need food to function, but we also use food to satisfy our cravings and other feelings. Going out for lunch or dinner is a way to relate to others and food accompanies many activities we do for entertainment. Food is a big part of our lives, but there are ways for us to sensibly shop for it.

- **Eat before you shop.** This applies to any shopping trip, but it's especially useful when food shopping. When we're hungry, our eyes are bigger than our stomachs and we will pick up everything we see. Those choices are inclined to be less healthy than normal. Hunger makes us impulsive and irrational, and those are two traits we don't need while shopping. Even if it's just a snack that can suppress your hunger pangs, it will increase your focus while in the grocery store.
- **Be prepared.** Make a list of the essential items you need and check it twice. A list keeps you on track and can help you tally your spending as you shop so that you stay on budget. Put snacks at the end of your list and only purchase them if your time and budget allow. If you shop at the same market frequently, map out your trip. Review the weekly sales circulars to see if the items you normally buy are discounted. Know exactly what aisles and sections you need to visit, and if you have a partner, split the list with them. The faster you complete your

list, the less likely you are to browse and buy unnecessary items. Finally, be a friend to the environment and take reusable bags with you to the store. It could even save you a few cents, depending on where you live.

- **Buy generic.** If you compare the name brand product to the generic or store brand product, you will likely find there is little difference in the taste and quality. Experiment with off-brand products to see if they stack up to your expectations. Switching at least some of your popular brand products to generic will save you money overall.

- **Buy certain staples in bulk.** Evaluate your refrigerator and shopping list while thinking about the meals you eat frequently. If there are certain food staples you consume frequently (like rice, sugar, flour, meat, and condiments), try to buy those in bulk. If your regular market doesn't offer bulk goods, check with your local warehouse store. They will likely require a membership, but you can borrow one from a friend or relative, purchase a temporary pass for the short-term, wait for a membership sale, or budget the membership cost into your spending plan. The money you save on purchasing some goods in bulk should pay for the membership over time.

- **Use a delivery service.** One way to avoid overspending and picking up food items you don't need is to have your groceries delivered to your home. All you need to do is submit your list to the site and pay, and they will do the shopping for you. Some grocery stores, such as Giant, provide this service directly, while other delivery services are managed by third-party companies like Instacart. There is a fee for the service, but when you consider the time, energy, and gas you would save by skipping the grocery store altogether, it might be worth it.

- **Prevent food waste.** Food waste equals money lost and more trips to the store to replace items. According to the Department of Agriculture, Americans waste $161 billion per year throwing out about one-third of their food. Understanding the manufacturing date labels on your food products is useful for decreasing food waste. The "sell by" date is for the grocery store. The "best by" or "use by date" is telling you the date until which the manufacturer guarantees the quality of the product; however, this information is not exact. Use your best judgment (and five senses) when inspecting a food item. You can also use an app, such as the FoodKeeper App recommended by the Food and Drug Administration, but more sensibly, eat the food that you buy in a timely manner. Make smaller meals and eat leftovers before cooking or buying new foods. Also, preserve and store your food properly. For example, cutting and jarring fresh fruits and vegetables can extend their life. Finally, don't overstuff your freezer, which can decrease its effectiveness in maintaining the temperature.

Purchasing Household Supplies

We need household supplies to maintain our homes. They are usually disposable items used by the entire family, such as toilet tissue, paper towels, trash bags, and dish soap. Like food and clothing, they're necessities you can't avoid buying, but the following are a few tips you can use to simplify your need for them.

- **Know your staples.** Similar to food, it's important to be aware of what you need and use the most, as well as the amount. How much toilet paper does your family go through in a month? How frequently do you clean your house? Make a list of all the supplies you use on a monthly basis. Also consider ways you can reduce the disposable impact of some supplies. Can you use cut-up old T-shirts as cleaning rags, reduce paper towel usage, or replace plastic sponges with biodegradable ones?

- **Buy in bulk and off-brand.** You will always need to replenish these items, so having consistent stock will reduce the number of trips to buy them. Buying in bulk reduces the cost per item, but you still need to be careful not to overbuy. Figure out the amount you need for a certain period of time, such as a month, and consider where you will store the products until you use all of them. Check to see what bulk items your local store carries and, if necessary, shop at a warehouse store, as recommended in the previous section. Again, compare the brands and test them out. If the cheaper generic or store brand version works just as well as the popular brand, save yourself a few cents and switch.

- **Find all-purpose supplies.** Certain natural cleaning agents—such as castile soap, borax, baking soda, and vinegar—are inexpensive and can clean many items and surfaces. For example, borax could be used to wash laundry and dishes. Stores also offer a variety of cleaning products marketed as all-purpose or multipurpose. If you can find a few staple cleaning products that work in multiple areas, you will save not only money but also storage space and additional trips to the store.

Shopping Mindfully

We've covered how to streamline your shopping for essentials such as clothing, food, and household supplies, but now let's consider some general ways to shop more mindfully. These tips are designed to deprioritize spending in some cases and give you more time and space to make intentional choices in others. Whenever you're looking for a simple way to check your spending, refer to the following strategies.

- **Adopt spend-free days.** Pick one day a week or a whole weekend to abstain from buying anything. Use this day to do something fun and free or use it as a day to review your budget and purchases from previous weeks. You could even challenge yourself to see how many spend-free days you can have in a month and how that impacts your budget.

- **Sleep on purchasing decisions.** When you see something you want to purchase, give yourself 24 hours or longer to think about the item. Intentionally consider the pros and cons of owning this product and if you absolutely need it. One of two things are likely to happen: 1) You'll forget about it or no longer want it. 2) You won't be able to stop thinking about it and you will find a justification for purchasing it. Either way, give yourself time to reduce impulsive purchases.

- **Give yourself a time frame while shopping.** Limit the amount of time you're in stores or shopping online. If you only need to purchase one item, give yourself ten minutes to do so. You will be less tempted to peruse the store for other things you don't need or see something on sale you must have. Set a timer on your phone and challenge yourself to beat it.

- **Spend money on experiences rather than objects.** When you get an unhealthy food craving or an urge to shop for nonessentials, think about an experience you want to have. Maybe you want to check out a new museum in your city or go to the spa for some relaxation. Experiences provide knowledge, adventures, and memories that physical items usually cannot. Think about your priorities and goals. Are they focused on having more experiences or buying more things?

- **Limit the amount of money you carry when out.** When shopping, only carry enough money for what you plan to purchase. Leave additional cash, credit cards, and debit cards at home or in a secure compartment in your vehicle, if you're concerned about emergencies.

If staying within your budget is a priority, you should carry cash more frequently because people tend to spend less money when they have cash than when paying with credit cards, according to several studies cited by Dr. Dholaki in *Psychology Today*.

- **Shop local.** Shopping local has many benefits. As opposed to shopping online, it supports your local economy and allows you to build relationships with local business owners. Getting to know the shop owners will increase your sense of community and could have long-term benefits for your shopping experience. Shopping in stores rather than online also lessens the negative impact on the environment by eliminating shipping, delivering, and additional packaging. While shopping local may limit the options you have compared to online shopping, it can be a practice in slow shopping and reducing your purchases. Shopping local keeps money circulating in your community, which can help improve available options and the quality of life in your city or town.

You now have strategies for simplifying your consumption habits when shopping for essential and general items. Clothing, food, and household supplies are things we have to shop for no matter our budgets, so it's important to streamline these activities as much as possible while still being mindful of how much we're spending. In this chapter, we learned how to simplify food shopping, and in the next chapter we'll concentrate on mindful eating and food preparation.

Chapter 8

Food and Diet

What and how we eat tells us a great deal about who we are. Food is representative of our culture, personal experiences, socioeconomic background, and health status. Food does not solely meet our physical needs—it also speaks to our mind-sets and feelings. In this chapter, we will get in touch with our food and examine that relationship in connection with our values and priorities.

Strategies for Simplifying Your Food and Diet

Take a moment to remind yourself of the top three priorities you chose to address with your food consumption. You can make notes about those priorities on the lines below. Finally, keep your *why* in mind and remember to stay present as you apply these strategies.

_____

_____

_____

Addressing Your Eating Habits

This can be a sensitive but necessary exercise. Examining the foods you eat and how you connect to them is key to creating a healthy and fulfilling relationship with food. Even generally healthy eaters can afford to take a closer look at their consumption patterns. Consider the following strategies when beginning to contend with your eating behavior.

- **Think about what you eat regularly.** Of the foods you eat daily and weekly, which do you consume most? Being aware of this information will help you later in the "Planning and Cooking Meals" section when you establish your go-to meals. Knowing what you eat all the time will also allow you to scrutinize the foods that are beneficial and the foods you can eliminate. Make a list of everything, including the beverages, you consume.

- **Analyze your relationship with food.** How does food make you feel? What were your experiences with food growing up? What memories are tied to food? What are your favorite foods and which do you dislike? Contemplate your history with food and how it impacts the connection you have with it today. Our relationship with food may be connected to our feelings about our bodies, too. These relationships can be complicated, but we can begin to simplify them by being aware. Practicing mindfulness gives us the space to observe our feelings about eating without judgment.

- **Understand the difference between diet and dieting.** Your diet is simply the food you eat, so following that logic, "dieting" simply means "eating." However, in American culture, the term "dieting" refers to restricting the amount or types of food one eats, usually with a goal of losing weight. Dieting in the United States is a culture and industry of its own, with endless types of diets and weight-loss products, some backed by research and others that are just trendy. Dieting culture has largely focused on weight loss with less of an emphasis on health. If you have a history of dieting, I'd like you to think about your experiences and how it makes you feel when the topic comes up. I also want you to keep in mind that your diet should support your lifestyle and add positively to your life. In this chapter, the goal is to simplify your diet, not by just eating less or eating only certain foods, but by making your eating experience integrated and fulfilling.

Eating Mindfully

Mindful eating asks us to focus on our food, to be aware of it and how it influences our well-being. Observing how you consume food, without judgment, along with the other strategies in this chapter, will give you the tools to successfully incorporate those small but practical changes in your eating habits that will have a significant impact on your lifestyle.

- **Eliminate distractions and savor your food.** Put your devices away, particularly your phone, and turn the television off. For the time that you're eating, focus on your food. If you're eating with your family or someone else, focus on them, too. Chew slowly and truly taste all the ingredients and flavors present in the food. Make every meal an experience.

- **Share meals.** When we share food with others, we can be more intentional about its enjoyment and preparation. Set aside time for meals, plan a special menu, or host a potluck. Use this time to not only nourish yourself and your loved ones, but also to connect with them. Sharing meals is a time-honored tradition in which people nurture bonds, create new relationships, do business, and plan for the future. Particularly if you live alone, make time in your schedule to connect with others over food at least once a month.

- **Read labels.** This is a strategy that will likely be used while shopping, but it's also an aspect of mindful eating. Knowing what you're putting into your body is important for developing a healthy relationship with food. Limit products that have too many ingredients and ones you can't pronounce or are unfamiliar with. Instead, look for and eat products with fewer overall ingredients and more natural and recognizable elements.

- **Express gratitude for your food.** This is not solely a spiritual practice but more so a values practice. Food is the fuel that powers our bodies and we can't live without it. The earth and farmers grow our food and companies process the raw ingredients into other foodstuffs we enjoy. Food scarcity is also a global epidemic. When consuming your food, pause for a moment to acknowledge your gratitude for the opportunity to nourish and sustain yourself and your family.

- **Choose quality over quantity.** Is your goal simply to eat or do you want to enjoy your food and feel satisfied? Choosing quality food and ingredients allows you to get the nutrients you need, enhance the taste of the food, and walk away from the table without hungering for more. Quality foods are usually fresh or raw, which means they are likely perishable; have vibrant colors, textures, and flavors; and are in season. The sources or production chain of quality foods can be easily identified, and if it's produced locally, that's even better. These are some ideas for judging the quality of foods, but it's important to determine your own standards and attain the highest quality you can afford. It may be a little more expensive, but it's likely worth it to your health and taste buds.

Planning and Cooking Meals

Meal preparation can consume much of our time and energy, particularly when we don't plan with purpose. Unless your plan is to purchase preprepared foods or eat at restaurants daily, which can take a huge hit on your wallet, most of us have to plan and cook our meals. The process does not have to be painstaking though. With a little mindfulness and the following tips, meal preparation will become a breeze.

- **Cook one-pot and one-pan meals.** Plan meals that can be cooked in one pot on the stove; in one electronic cooking pot, such as a Crock-Pot; or in one pan or dish in the oven. You will not have to continuously monitor the food and will be free to relax or do something else. There are tons of one-pot meal recipes on Pinterest and other cooking sites if you need ideas. Also, many of these meals include high amounts of vegetables and protein sources to sustain your energy.

- **Eat smaller but more frequent meals.** Rather than focusing on preparing three large meals per day, entertain the idea of consuming smaller meals throughout the day. The size of the meals can be moderately sized (larger than a snack but smaller than your normal meal) and you can consume about five or more of these smaller meals in a day. Recent research reported by CNN has shown that adopting this eating pattern can boost your metabolism and regulate cholesterol and insulin levels. Ultimately, you should consult with your doctor before making any major changes, but switching up your eating schedule might allow you to reset your habits.

- **Try meatless meals or entire days.** Decreasing our meat consumption is great for our health because meat contains fat and cholesterol. It is also helpful to our budgets because meat is often one of the more expensive items when we food shop. Meals without meat are generally quicker to prepare, too, leaving us with more family time or personal time. Preparing meatless meals on a regular basis is also beneficial to the environment. The toll of raising livestock—including the contamination of air, water, and land—has been well-documented in a recent 2018 study published in *Nature* journal.

- **Establish your go-to recipes and eat them frequently.** In the "Addressing Your Eating Habits" section, I asked you to consider the foods you eat regularly. Think back to those ingredients and choose what meals you enjoy making with them. Record the meals and their recipes, and now you've created your own personalized menu. Stop fretting over what to fix for every meal and refer to your menu. Trying to vary our meals too often only introduces stress and expense into our lives.

- **Identify and stock your ingredient staples.** If you're going to eat the same foods and meals regularly, as suggested in the previous strategy, it is crucial to make sure you always have those ingredients on hand and that the food is flavorful. Eating tasty food staves off the potential boredom of eating the same thing routinely, and having your staples in stock lessens the temptation to do unplanned food shopping, eat at restaurants, or order delivery. Keep a list in the kitchen of all your staples, including spices, so it's handy when you're ready to shop.

- **Prepare your meals in advance.** Spend less time planning and preparing your meals by prepping them at the beginning of the week. You can fully cook meals for the week and apportion them for each day, or you can do all the food prep—such as cutting fruits and vegetables, soaking beans, and marinating meat—for the meals you're planning to prepare throughout the week. Either way, having some type of plan for the week and doing some preparation work can simplify the cooking process and reduce frustration.

Organizing Your Kitchen

Having an organized kitchen supports making simplified meals. Kitchens can be one of the most cluttered spaces in our homes because of the stunning variety of items found in them. They're one of the areas we use daily, which means this space constantly needs to be cleaned and maintained.

- **Determine your essential kitchen appliances.** Before you declutter your kitchen, create a list of your most-used appliances. When thinking about the type of meals you prepare frequently, narrow down those appliances to your must-have equipment and eliminate the rest during your kitchen declutter. If there is an item you want to acquire to simplify meal preparation, check out thrift stores to see if you can find it in good condition and at a significantly reduced price than buying new.

- **Declutter kitchen tools, your pantry, and your refrigerator.** Audit and declutter all your utensils, appliances, dishes, pots, and pans. Go through your refrigerator and freezer and dispose of old or expired foods and beverages. After removing those items, do a deep clean of the refrigerator. You can save space in your refrigerator by placing some fruits and vegetables on the counter or dining table. After decluttering the pantry, you can donate foodstuffs that are unopened and unexpired to organizations that provide food to homeless and low-income people. For cabinets and cupboards with dishes, figure out how many pieces each person needs in your home. For example, perhaps you only need two complete sets of dishes.

- **Make everything accessible.** Decluttering will assist with this task by reducing the amount of items overall and making you aware of what you have. Make sure that the items you use—such as dishes, appliances, and tools—can be quickly found by you and your family. Place fresh fruits on the counter or table so that you can grab a healthy snack without thinking. Store your beans and other dry goods in clear containers so that you remember you have them and can monitor the amount. Arrange your spices in a spice rack or in an area near your stove, though not directly above the stove because constant exposure to heat will cause them to degrade. The more you're aware of what you have, the more you will use it.

- **Use your dining table.** Not only can you store fruits and vegetables on your table, but it can also be a place for quality time during meals and meal planning. Remove anything from the table that is not related to eating and the kitchen. This is especially useful if you're limited on space. Chop vegetables, create and review your grocery and household shopping lists, talk about meals and plan menus for the upcoming weeks, and, of course, eat at your table whenever possible. Establish your dining table as an integral part of the kitchen experience.

Tackling your food and diet may have been challenging, but I hope you now have a practical game plan to help you be more cognizant about what goes into your body, the maintenance and storage of this important resource, and how your habits can align with your chosen priorities. Next, we'll examine another sensitive topic: our relationships. The people we engage with and how we interact with them plays an important role in our quality of life.

Chapter 9

—

Relationships

We engage in many interpersonal relationships throughout our lives. Besides our partners, children, and close family members, we form connections with friends, extended family, coworkers, and acquaintances, among others. These relationships include different levels of communication, sharing, and commonalities. Relationships can be complicated because they involve the exchange of ideas and emotions, but they don't have to be. You can simplify your relationships, just as you have worked on simplifying the other areas of your life.

Strategies for Simplifying Your Relationships

Before we discuss how to simplify your relationships, think about the top three priorities you chose for relationships in chapter 2. Feel free to make notes about those priorities on the write-on lines below if it's helpful and keep in mind your *why* and your values as you think about them. Remember to stay present as you apply these strategies.

_____

_____

_____

Addressing Your Current Relationships

Take some time to examine the relationships in your life. In this section, we'll identify who those people are and understand why you've connected with them and how you've engaged with them over the years. This information will help you determine what you want your relationships to look like going forward.

- **Think about the people in your life.** Sit down and list all the people you have a relationship with. Try to remember as many names as possible and note how they are connected to you (for example, friend, relative, coworker, etc.). Do not ask anyone for help with this exercise because it's key to see who is noted and who is not. Take stock of who is in your life. For the people you're able to list and remember, we will investigate those relationships further to determine if they are needed and how to make them more mindful. For the people who are forgotten, that speaks to their importance in your life.

- **Consider the best and worst relationship you've experienced.** Think about all the relationships you just listed for a moment. Consider the qualities of these relationships. What makes them fulfilling or undesirable? Put a plus sign next to the ones that rise to the top and a minus sign next to the ones that sink to the bottom. Knowing this information gives you a barometer for gauging your relationships and lets you know what to attract more of and what to avoid. Throughout the remainder of this chapter, I'll ask you to consider this list as you work through the strategies for different relationships.

- **Determine the values you prioritize in a relationship.** Clear your mind of everything we just discussed and think about what you look for in a relationship. What are the minimum requirements, nonnegotiables, and worthy characteristics that should be present in your connections? What are your needs and wants in a relationship? Think about your personal values and the priorities you chose for this section to help you determine your relationship values.

- **Understand the love languages.** According to author Gary Chapman, there are five primary love languages that we express: verbal affirmation, acts of service, quality time, receiving gifts, and physical touch. We all have one central love language and a secondary one. Knowing your love language helps you communicate to people how you want to be celebrated and acknowledged. You should also learn the love languages of the people you interact with in order to show them gratitude and acknowledgment. You can take the quiz and share it with others by going to 5LoveLanguages.com. Relationships are a two-way street, so in addition to knowing what you need in a relationship, it's important to let others know that you care for them and value what they contribute.

- **Write difficult feelings before sharing.** If you need to have an uncomfortable conversation with someone, try writing your thoughts and feelings before sharing them. After you've written them, allow your thoughts to marinate for a night or two. We can cause unnecessary conflicts by speaking our minds about something complex in the moment. Use what you've learned about mindfulness and explore why you may feel upset before sharing it with the other party or parties.

- **Declutter your relationships.** Now that you've analyzed your relationships, what you value in them, what you need from them, and how you love and support the people you connect with, it's time to release some of those associations that don't bring you joy and are simply taking up space in your life. Go through your list again, looking especially closely at the ones you marked with a minus sign, and begin to tease out those unwanted relationships. This is also a good time to think about the relationships you want to stay in, but which might need some work to improve them. Finally, for the relationships that are great and meet your expectations, make a simple plan to reach out to those people and let them know you appreciate them.

Balancing Extended Family

Your immediate family is generally your spouse, children, parents, siblings, grandparents or grandchildren, and even in-laws. Your extended family consists of aunts, uncles, cousins, and distant relatives. While these are acceptable definitions of immediate and extended families, what you have experienced growing up and how you view family now could be different. For the purposes of this section, we'll think of extended family as any relatives we don't have regular contact with and only see occasionally. You can think about how you define extended family and how you positioned those individuals in the previous section.

- **Create a family tree.** It doesn't have to be too complex but can be a simple spreadsheet or list, or you can use a website like Ancestry.com or MyHeritage.com to create a digital tree. Knowing who is in your family and how you're related is interesting and useful information to have and share with family members. Your family history can also be passed down to your children and grandchildren. If you don't know a lot about your family history, this is a good opportunity to spend some quality time with the older generations and history keepers in your family. You may also want to add contact information such as phone numbers, e-mail addresses, and mailing addresses to your tree to keep in touch and send out cards or announcements for special occasions.

- **Make extended family time a priority.** Because we typically don't see extended family as often as immediate family, make it a point to attend big family events at least a few times per year. For the family you marked with a plus sign, absolutely make the effort to attend those gatherings. For those you marked with a minus sign, you need to weigh if you're willing to sacrifice your peace to maintain those bonds. Enter these gathering dates into your calendar and decide which ones you will attend. If family gatherings are too few and far between, consider planning a reunion with the help of other relatives. Again, a gathering doesn't have to be a complex affair. A simple potluck dinner or picnic in the park is a wonderful way to connect. The most important thing is spending quality time together.

- **Balance multiple extended families.** Many of us have several family groups from our mother's and father's sides, and if you're partnered, you likely have in-laws. Deciding where to go for the holidays and other special events can be overwhelming, especially if you don't want to miss anyone. Find out as much information as possible in advance about each family's plans, make a list of all events, and then choose which you will attend. You don't have to go to every function if you don't want to, but plan to attend at least one gathering of each family throughout the year. If you can't or choose not to attend, contact the organizers to let them know and send your well wishes so that your family knows you're thinking of them. During big holiday vacations, spread out who you visit over the weeks or months.

- **Create a family Facebook group.** If most of your family uses Facebook, you may want to organize a family page or chat messenger group. You can make the group private, and members will have the ability to share news, information, and pictures with everyone. Each person can set personal preferences for commenting and notifications. While this is not a substitute for in-person time, it can fill in the gaps between gatherings and help everyone stay linked.

- **Accept your family without compromising your priorities and values.** It's difficult to "declutter" family ties because we don't get a say in who our blood family is. Regardless of the quality of the relationships, we can feel obligated to maintain these ties from internal guilt or pressure from others. With that being said, you have to further refine who is a priority within your family. While you didn't choose your family, you still have a choice about the relationships you want in your life. Consider how to best engage with everyone based on the strategies provided, but if certain relationships hold little value or are too toxic, by all means, keep your distance from those relatives.

Maintaining Friendships

Friends are our chosen family and they hold a special space in our hearts. Friends are different from family because they usually come into our lives based on shared experiences and commonalities. Friends may be the people we turn to when we need a break from our other relationships or they could be our primary relationships. With that in mind, recall your friendships from the list in the first section and let's explore some strategies for developing simple and sustainable friendships.

- **Know that it's okay to have different types of friends.** I would actually encourage you to cultivate relationships with people based on your varied interests. Your different friend groups also don't need to be friends with each other. You may have friends who you grew up with, went to college with, share a hobby with, like to go to happy hour with, or are neighbors with. Allow those folks to fulfill these different roles so that no one person or friend group is responsible for meeting all your needs and wants.

- **Don't get caught up on minor conflicts and differences.** No one sees eye to eye on everything all the time. Don't allow a minor situation to become a big one and potentially destroy a good friendship. Most conflicts come from misunderstandings. Pause mindfully to decide if the issue is really worth pursuing. If you feel it is, ask for clarification first before taking a position. If, after careful thought, you realize it's not a serious issue, let it go. Don't address it further unless your friend feels differently. However, if you have friends who are constant sources of conflict and ranked near the bottom of your list, it's probably time to terminate those friendships.

- **Evaluate your friendships.** Periodically, take some time to contemplate your current friendships. We collect friends from different phases of our lives, and we may find we've grown apart from some of our friends. You may no longer have the things in common you had when you originally met. It's okay to let some friendships go or demote them to acquaintances or to social media friends. You can quietly walk away without announcing it, if you feel that's appropriate. If you were once very close and are not now, you may want to address the situation. It's possible these friends have noticed the difference, too. Wish these types of friends well from afar and free up any mental or emotional space they were holding. Thinning out toxic or unnecessary friendships leaves more space to strengthen the healthy ones.

- **Be flexible with your friends.** They likely also have full schedules, juggling a multitude of relationships, careers, and home lives. Be considerate of both your and their time. If they can't get a babysitter, offer to spend time with them in their home. If their lives are feeling hectic, offer to run errands together. We make the time for the people we care about. This strategy applies to communication, too. Texting may be seen as informal communication, but a "thinking of you" or "just checking in" text can go a long way to sustaining a friendship when you're not able to see each other in person. If you're repeatedly finding it difficult to spend time with certain friends, you may need to reconsider where they fall on your list of relationships.

- **Pencil them in.** You have family, personal, and work commitments designated on your calendars, so make space for your friends, too. Putting them on your calendar is an intentional step to show they matter. If you treat your meet up with your friend like an important appointment, you'll be less likely to forget and it can give you something to look forward to throughout the week or month. Don't forget to add their birthdays and anniversaries to your calendar so that you can wish them well.
- **Ask questions.** This strategy applies to all relationships. The people you interact with want to know you're interested in them, and one of the best and simplest ways to do this is to ask them questions about what's going on in their lives. This is especially helpful if they're telling you about something that is important to them, but it can also be used as a conversation starter to check in with someone you care about. The questions can be as simple as "What did you do today?", "How is work going?", or "How was your weekend?" Ask follow-up questions about previous conversations, such as "Is your mother feeling better?" or "How was your doctor's appointment?"

Interacting with Acquaintances and Coworkers

Acquaintances are people we don't have an established relationship with. We see them at events and different activities. They could be friends of other people you associate with or just people you happen to see at your weekly yoga class. You greet them and make small talk, but it rarely goes beyond that, though you might be friends on social media. Acquaintances are the relationships that are easiest to simplify because there is little investment in them. In contrast, we see our coworkers almost as often as our families, though they could still only be acquaintances. Coworking relationships can become complicated when professional lines are blurred and coworkers become friends. While developing deeper bonds with your coworkers can be beneficial to the work environment, it's important to ensure these relationships fulfill their first purpose: accomplishing the work. Where did your acquaintances and coworkers fall on your list? Did they even make the list? Consider these questions as you review the following strategies.

- **Go with the flow.** If you're happy with the casual relationships you currently have, there's nothing you need to do and there is no pressure to develop the relationship into true friendships. With coworkers who are not your friends, just stick to business as usual within working hours.

- **Contact them through public forums.** If you're connected to your acquaintances through social media and need to contact them for some reason, send them a message online. There's no need to exchange your personal contact information if you have no intention of building a relationship with them. You can also contact coworkers through official work channels, when necessary.

- **Feel them out.** If you decide you're interested in getting to know an acquaintance or coworker better, the next time you see them, set a date to meet in a different environment, perhaps to grab coffee or have lunch together. Make the date low-commitment, meaning that it's fine if someone has to cancel. Have a conversation and see if you have any commonalities. If it doesn't feel like a match, simply go back to your normal behavior.

- **Set boundaries between your personal and work life.** This is especially important if your personal life could have a negative impact on your work. Decide how much personal information you want to share with coworkers, particularly if they rank near the bottom of your relationship list or didn't make it on the list at all. Consider if you would invite them to social functions outside of work or keep in touch if one of you moved on from the company. Additionally, think twice about being friends with your colleagues on social media. This is another area where professional and personal lines can blur.

- **Attend company social functions intentionally.** Participating in work-sponsored social events can help reinforce your work relationships and establish you as a team player. While it may be important to attend some events, choose them wisely. Go to events where your presence can have the most impact or where the atmosphere is mainly casual. Unless they're mandatory, you don't need to attend every event, especially if you have other personal and familial obligations that are higher priorities.

Managing Your Social Media

Social media can serve as an extension of your in-person relationships. They are also platforms where acquaintances and other casual relationships can begin to form.

The downside of social media is that it can be a huge drain on our time and can lead us to believe that we have closer relationships with some people than we actually do. Use the strategies below to keep your social media connections simple and appropriate.

- **Conduct a social media sweep.** Declutter your social media friends or followers. Delete contacts you don't know, can't remember, don't like, have no communication with, and compare yourself to. Also, feel free to delete contacts who share negative information and who over-post. Feel free to release anyone, for any reason you feel is legitimate. If you feel uncomfortable deleting someone, you can block or mute them so that you still appear to be connected but their posts won't appear on your feed. Conduct these sweeps periodically to stay on top of who you receive information from and who can view your posts.
- **Use your privacy settings.** You can control how much of your information is shared with different groups of people. You can also control who is allowed to see your profile and who can request you as a connection. If you're friends online with distant relatives, coworkers, or acquaintances, this is a great way to limit their access to what you post.

- **Reduce notifications.** Determine what types of notifications, if any, you want to receive. This can include new posts from friends, game and app requests, and comment alerts. If constant notifications distract or annoy you, limiting them can go a long way toward protecting your peace of mind and keeping a positive opinion of your online friends, especially those who post frequently.
- **Do not allow social media to replace real-life connections.** While social media is a useful way to keep up with the developments in the lives of your family and friends, especially when they're not local, it can't substitute for in-person bonding and quality time. Follow up with your loved ones offline when they share important information and make reasonable attempts to be present for major life events and celebrations whenever possible.
- **Think before you post.** If you're sharing potentially sensitive or controversial information on your social media accounts, think about the impact it can have on your online and offline worlds. While you have the right to share anything you want, as long as it doesn't violate the platform's community standards, some posts still may not be a good idea. Write out what you

plan to post first, read over it, and verify the sources of information. Also, if you're sharing important information about yourself online, share it privately with your close friends and those at the top of your list first. Would you want your loved ones to learn something personal about you from social media?

In this chapter, we reviewed the different types of relationships we encounter outside of our immediate family and strategies for simplifying those connections. You also had the opportunity to identify and position those relationships. The common themes throughout these strategies are to communicate effectively and appropriately, show up and be present, create boundaries, and be flexible when necessary. Relationships can require a large amount of time, so it's important to remain aware of the priorities you chose for this area as we move into the next chapter where we'll focus on your personal use of time.

Chapter 10

—

Time
Management

Time is one of our most valuable
resources and it's finite, meaning
you can't produce more of it once
it's been used. Your time is valuable
because you are valuable. Learning
to manage your time effectively and
focus your energy on the things that
matter most to you is a significant
step toward simplifying your life. We
all want more time, but we simply
need to understand how to use the
time we have more efficiently.

Strategies for Simplifying Your Time Management

Take some time to recall the top three priorities you chose in chapter 2 regarding your time. Make notes about them on the lines below, if necessary. As you consider those priorities, also keep in mind your *why* and your values. Remember to stay present as you work through these strategies.

_____

_____

_____

Addressing Your Time Usage

Many of us are unable to recall where all our time goes. We do know that time seems to pass quickly as we age and as we look back over our lives. Besides work and major life events, it can be difficult to pinpoint what else we've been doing. In this section, you'll reevaluate how you spend your time so that you can better focus on your priorities.

- **Track your time for several days.** If you're feeling ambitious, do this for a week, using pen and paper or a note-taking app. Break up your days into blocks, perhaps two hours at a time, from when you wake up until you go to bed. Record as much information as possible about getting dressed, eating meals, commuting, working, taking breaks, running errands, relaxing, spending time on social media, daydreaming, and any other activities. Be sure to also note the next morning how many hours you slept. Review all your notes and look for patterns. When are you most and least productive? How do you relax? How much time do you spend scrolling online? How much time do you spend at your desk or in your vehicle? Do you hit the snooze button or fall asleep with the television on? Are you sleeping enough? Not only should you take note of what you're doing, but you should also notice what may be missing.

- **Empty your plate.** Now that you've had the opportunity to analyze what you do daily, you can declutter some of the commitments and activities that drain your time. Be ruthless in eliminating the things that take up time but don't add value to your life. Recall your top priorities as you consider what you want for your new simplified life.

- **Consider the access others have to you.** Review the log you kept and identify the activities that involve others, including your employer. Compared to the time you spend doing things alone, are you giving more of yourself to others than you should? If that's the case, revisit chapter 9 to figure out a plan to prioritize your relationships without deprioritizing yourself. Where can you give yourself more time?

- **Track your vacation and sick time for the year.** If you need data on your leave time, visit your company's human resources department and have them pull a report for you. You can request the current year and the past couple of years to establish your leave habits. I encourage you to use your days off engaging in activities that benefit your relaxation and wellness. If it's challenging to take time off right now, inquire about compensation for any unused vacation or personal days. If this is not a policy at your company, then I implore you to use the leave time you have earned. Prioritize yourself by creating a balance between *you* time and work time.

- **Set boundaries between yourself and the other areas of your life.** Establish clear confines between your personal time, family time, social time, and work time. Designate separate times and spaces for these areas whenever possible.

Prioritizing "You Time" and Self-Care

Devoting time to yourself is paramount to self-development. You learn so much about yourself when you spend time alone, including what you need, what you want, and what you're capable of. "You time" is also important for self-care, which is necessary to replenish your energy, restore your mental capacities, and relax. The following are strategies for focusing on yourself.

- **Schedule time for yourself.** Spend some time scheduling all activities that pertain to your happiness, health, and well-being. Book your annual check-ups and dentist appointments, therapy sessions, beauty appointments, and fitness classes. Make sure to carve out time for leisure activities—such as catching a movie—and relaxation activities—such as naps or meditation. Also, schedule time where you have absolutely nothing planned. Use this time to do nothing or go on an unplanned adventure. Make this time nonnegotiable.
- **Find a passion or hobby you enjoy.** Perhaps it's an activity you did as a child that you want to revisit or a new craft you'd like to learn. Find an activity that both excites and challenges you and commit to it. Whether it's for

fun or something you want to master, show up consistently and practice mindfulness during the activity.

- **Give yourself an experience instead of an object.** Many people view self-care and self-reward as a time to buy themselves something. It could be something they've wanted for a long-time or a frivolous item they buy just because they can. While there is nothing wrong with buying yourself something occasionally, remember your home and shopping priorities and think about a memory you can create instead. Perhaps you've always wanted to take a solo travel trip or go to a concert or festival alone. Or perhaps it's something as simple as watching the sunset in reflective silence.

- **Don't be afraid to say "no."** You don't have to accept every invitation or request for your time. Saying "no" can be extremely challenging, especially for people who like to please others. Don't allow your discomfort or the emotions of others to influence you. Be mindful of them and state your priorities if you wish, though you don't owe anyone an explanation or your time. Saying "no" is like exercising a muscle: You have to flex it to build its strength over time. Learning how to refuse requests that aren't aligned with your values and priorities will make the times when you say "yes" more meaningful.

- **Keep "you time" sacred.** Limit people's access to you while you're spending time with yourself. Decrease the methods people can use to contact you, including putting your phone on the "do not disturb" setting or leaving it in another room. Block out any distractions and only give people enough information to reach you in an emergency. Lock doors, ignore entreaties, and generally make yourself unavailable during your alone time.

- **Check in with yourself.** Ask yourself, "Am I okay?", "Am I happy?", "Do I have everything I need?", and "What am I working toward?" These questions can be difficult, but they are crucial to answer. You need to be able to assess how you're doing. If you're not doing well or think you could use some help accessing and sorting through your thoughts and emotions, consider contacting a counselor or therapist. Mental health is one area where we don't always follow up the way we do with our physical health. Contact your insurance company to see what providers are in your network or reach out to your local mental health department to see what services are available.

Manage Your Personal Calendar

We've talked about the value of creating calendars and scheduling essential tasks and events throughout this book, and your personal time is no exception. Prioritize your personal time to the same degree you prioritize your work, social, and family commitments. The strategies in this section may sound similar to those from those other sections because they're essential regardless of the situation.

- **Break up your days into blocks.** Batching your day can also work for your personal schedule. Review the exercise from the "Addressing Your Time Usage" section in which you tracked your time and think about how you want your day to flow. Identify blocks of time where you can exercise, run errands, work on hobbies, or relax and watch your favorite show. Look for areas on your calendar where you will not be interrupted, if practical. Additionally, while blocking your day, make use of the timer function on your phone or use a stopwatch. This will help you be aware of how long common activities generally take and ensure you're engaged for a sufficient amount of time.
- **Review your schedule for the next day before going to sleep.** It only takes five minutes or less to do this

and it helps you wake up feeling prepared for what the day holds. Surveying your calendar the night before will also give you the opportunity to do any necessary preparations, such as pulling out important documents or setting your alarm a bit earlier so that you're not scrambling and flustered in the morning. The attitude you start your day with can influence the rest of your day.

- **Sleep on invitations before making a decision.** Similar to giving yourself time before making purchases, do the same with invitations and other requests. Take a full 24 hours or several days before committing your time and yourself to someone else. Ask follow-up questions about the event and what is expected of you, and confirm the request will not interfere with any other events on your schedule. This strategy will also help you avoid overcommitting yourself.
- **Wake up earlier to accomplish more.** If there is something you want to achieve in your personal life, it requires you to be more intentional about how you spend your time. While it's tempting to sleep in on days when you don't have family and work responsibilities, if you occasionally wake up even one hour earlier, you can commit that time to a goal. Rising earlier may also

allow you to have some "you time" before your partner or children wake up. If it is too challenging to get up earlier on workdays, try this on the weekends and see how it goes. Rising earlier can eventually become part of your daily routine. Naturally, waking up earlier will prompt you to want to go to sleep earlier in the evening, as well. However, if you are more productive in that early uninterrupted hour than you would be late at night, going to bed a little earlier is a positive change to your routine.

Browsing the Internet

One of the major ways we lose time is by being online. Though the Internet and its associated technologies and applications are integral parts of our lives in the twenty-first century, they need moderation like everything else we consume. In fact, you can even use some of this technology to simplify your Internet usage.

- **Track your screen time.** Do you know how much time you spend online? The Internet can be accessed via our smartphones, computers, tablets, and smart televisions, and we use the Internet at work, school, and home. We are virtually connected to the Internet at all times. Fortunately, you can easily keep track of your time spent online. Apple users can utilize the Screen Time function found in the settings of their iPhones and tablets and computer, laptop, and Android users can download apps to their devices that will track their time. These functions will allow you to see how much time you're connected and set limits on your daily use. You can manage these settings for yourself and everyone in your household.

- **Be conscious of what you're consuming.** Not all news and information is reliable or accurate. Anyone can publish just about anything online, and it has become more difficult to distinguish fake-news websites from legitimate ones. Take note of your emotional and mental states as you browse and after you're finished. Do you feel energized or drained? Inspired or defeated? If you feel drained and defeated, now is a good time to change what you're viewing. Through your Internet browser settings, you have the power to block websites and protect your privacy. Also, make sure to verify information you read by cross-checking it with several reputable sources.
- **Be mindful of what personal information is available online.** Periodically, search for yourself on Google or another search engine to see what comes up. If you find anything troublesome, do your best to locate the author and have it removed. The information or

images may appear on your own social media sites, so remove anything you don't want people to see and adjust your privacy settings. Additionally, to avoid being hacked, change your passwords at least once per year and be wary of using the same password for multiple online accounts.

- **Institute Internet-free or tech-free days.** You can start with a few waking hours and work your way up to a full day. Once you pick a day, plan fun activities to fill your time. Maybe visit a state park or beach, take a painting class, or assemble a 500-piece puzzle. As you discover Internet-free activities that are free or low-cost to do at home or locally, keep a list for future reference. Try scheduling one day per month sans Internet and devices and then add more days if everything goes well.

Your time is precious, and you should honor and protect it at all costs. If you look back through the previous chapters, you can see that how you spend your time is connected to every area of your life and your priorities. Even as you address those spaces, it's important to remember to set aside time that is only for you. We have covered all the essential topics you need to simplify your life, and in the final chapter, I will offer you strategies to maintain this lifestyle.

Chapter 11

———

Sticking with It

Congratulations on making it this far and gaining so many useful strategies to guide you on your journey to simplicity. When we started this journey in chapter 1, I advised you that the term "simple" does not always mean "easy." While the tips provided are actionable and practical, they will only work if you routinely practice mindfulness and follow through on the methods presented in this book. It takes willpower to adapt to this simplified lifestyle, and I'll leave you with ten useful strategies to stay the course when it feels too challenging to continue.

Strategies for Staying the Course

- **Remember that you're enough and you're capable.** You already have everything you need within you to make these changes. You're aware of your priorities and you know how to apply mindful simplicity to your actions. I'm sure you've made big changes and survived difficult times before, and the good news is that simplifying your life will probably be a lot easier to accomplish. Have confidence in your ability to do what needs to be done.

- **Pause, breathe, and be present.** In chapter 2, we discussed how staying present is a powerful tool and the most crucial strategy to master before the others. Being present in the moment puts life into perspective and allows you to focus on the current challenge. Whenever you feel discomfort or obstacles arising, don't give into the negativity. Take a moment to recenter yourself and then recall your priorities.

- **Keep a gratitude journal.** When we start to release things from our lives, particularly things we've held on to for a long time, it can feel as though we're losing parts of ourselves. In this case, remember the first strategy on this list: "You are enough." Then spend some time thinking about what you still have that you're grateful for. Contemplate the things that you have the power to hold on to forever, such as your values. Also, as you're letting go of things, express gratitude for how they have served you up to this point, which is a practice that professional organizer Marie Kondo recommends. Consider what you can welcome into your life with the time and space you're gaining by letting these habits and objects go.

- **Find an accountability partner and make your priorities visible.** Sometimes we need support on our journey to reach the next level. There may be someone who is also on a simplicity journey or just someone you feel is good at providing assistance and encouragement. This person should be reliable and have time to help you when needed. If you don't have anyone in your life who can hold you accountable, create your own accountability system. Ensure that your priorities are always visible and accessible by saving them to your devices, making them your screensaver, or posting them wherever you know you will see them regularly. Use the technological tools we discussed in the previous chapters to set reminders and track your activities.

- **Manage expectations and allow yourself to fail.** You have expectations for yourself, and others may hold expectations for you, too. Set realistic goals and timelines. You can inform others—such as your accountability partner and family—of your plans, but don't allow anyone else's expectations for you to dictate what you're doing or make you feel inadequate. Despite your best efforts, some strategies and projects will not pan out like you expected. It's okay to allow yourself a loss periodically. If you experience failure, instead of getting upset or letting it derail your journey, approach the loss mindfully and learn from it. Look for the lessons in everything and don't stress about the small stuff. If your goal was to eliminate 10 items but you only got rid of five, you still have five fewer items than when you started, which is progress.
- **Update your priorities.** Life is always changing whether we recognize it or not. Some changes are planned, some are surprises, and some occur naturally over time. If your priorities no longer fit with your reality, you can reprioritize them. Return to chapter 2 and choose new priorities that are aligned with your current life. It may also be necessary to redefine your values, goals,

needs, and wants over time. Remember that you determine and define your values, priorities, and goals.

- **Pick the easiest task when you feel stuck.** Sometimes the task before us can seem overwhelming and too difficult to accomplish in the moment. When a situation like this comes along, break the project down into smaller tasks and choose the easiest one to do right now. Completing a small task is still an accomplishment and will move you forward. Also remember that "done is better than perfect." Don't let the need to be perfect stall you. You can always improve on what you've done, but you can't improve on nothing.

- **Do one thing at a time.** Similar to the previous strategy, if you feel burdened by everything you feel you have to do, just start with one thing. It can be the easiest or the hardest thing. Doing the hardest thing first allows you to devote fresh energy to solving the problem and makes it more likely you will complete it. Have you ever tried to do a difficult task at the end of the day when you're tired? It can feel impossible. No matter what you choose to do, keep in mind that you only have to do one thing right now.

- **Create a "to-don't" list.** You know what your priorities are and what you need to do to meet them, but have you stopped to think about what you absolutely don't want in your life? Make a list of all the things you don't need, want, or like and will not do under any circumstances. Know what you will not negotiate. Having a list of "Hard Nos" will help you avoid bringing unnecessary clutter into your life in the future.

- **Reread this book.** I've referred to chapters and sections throughout this book because they really do contain helpful information and tips. Review the strategies as often as needed and incorporate them into your life. Bookmark the things that really stand out to you and share them with others, if you feel it will help them, too. Anytime you need to refresh or restart your simplicity journey, this book will be here for you.

We've reached the end of our journey together. We've explored all the major areas of your life and the practical ways to simplify them. We've also learned about the cultural significance of pursuing a simple life and the power of mindfulness in decluttering our lives. I want to reiterate that you're capable and have everything you need to create the life you desire. Thank you for allowing me to be your guide, and remember that I'm here to assist you whenever you need me.

Resources

Please consider the following resources to further your understanding of simplicity and assist you on your journey.

READ

Newport, Cal. *Digital Minimalism: Choosing a Focused Life in a Noisy World.* Portfolio, February 5, 2019.

McKeown, Greg. *Essentialism: The Disciplined Pursuit of Less.* Currency, April 15, 2014.

Kondo, Marie. *The Life Changing Magic of Tidying Up: The Japanese Art of Decluttering and Organizing.* Ten Speed Press, October 14, 2014.

Layne, Erica. *The Minimalist Way: Minimalism Strategies to Declutter Your Life and Make Room for Joy.* Althea Press, March 12, 2019.

Boyle, Erin. *Simple Matters: Living with Less and Ending Up with More.* Harry N. Abrams, January 12, 2016.

WATCH

Layne, Erica. "10 Outstanding TED Talks to Inspire You to Live Simply". May 17, 2018. www.ericalayne.co /10-outstanding-ted-talks-live-simply/.

D'Avella, Mike. *Minimalism: A Documentary About the Important Things.* The Minimalists, LLC. 2016.

The Story of Stuff Project. *The Story of Stuff.* April 22, 2009. www.youtube.com/watch?v=9GorqroigqM.

Kondo, Marie. *Tidying Up with Marie Kondo.* Netflix. January 1, 2019. www.netflix.com/title/80209379.

GO

Earth911.com

The Arc.org

Goodwill Donation Centers

Habitat for Humanity ReStore

Salvation Army Donation Centers

References

Abrams, Allison, LCSW-R. "Mental Health and the Effects of Social Media." *Psychology Today*. March 5, 2017. www.psychologytoday.com/gb/blog/nurturing-self -compassion/201703/mental-health-and-the-effects -social-media.

Boss, Shira. "What Your Stuff Is Costing You." *AARP*. January 3, 2018. www.aarp.org/money/budgeting-saving/info-2018 /clutter-cost-fd.html.

Brahm, Chris, Greg Caimi, and Micheal Mankins. "Your Scarcest Resource." *Harvard Business Review*. May 2014. www.hbr.org /2014/05/your-scarcest-resource.

Bureau of Labor Statistics. "100 Years of U.S. Consumer Spending." U.S. Department of Labor. May 2006. www.bls.gov/opub /100-years-of-u-s-consumer-spending.pdf.

Carrington, Damian. "Huge Reduction in Meat-Eating 'Essential' to Avoid Climate Breakdown." *The Guardian*. October 10, 2018. www.theguardian.com/environment/2018/oct/10/huge -reduction-in-meat-eating-essential-to-avoid-climate -breakdown.

Department of Agriculture. "Frequently Asked Questions." Accessed July 8, 2019. www.usda.gov/oce/foodwaste /faqs.htm.

Dholaki, Uptal. Ph.D. "Does It Matter Whether You Pay with Cash or a Credit Card?" Psychology Today. July 11, 2016. www.psychologytoday.com/us/blog/the-science-behind -behavior/201607/does-it-matter-whether-you-pay-cash -or-credit-card.

Dietrich, Cindy. "Decision Making: Factors that Influence Decision Making, Heuristics Used, and Decision Outcomes." *Student Pulse, 2*(02). 2010. Accessed June 19, 2019. https://pdfs.semanticscholar.org/b496/716cb15fcd7193 aaa7f199ed614b1d7e57fc.pdf.

Drayer, Lisa. "Should You Eat Three Big Meals or Many Mini Meals?" *CNN*. June 2, 2017. www.cnn.com/2017/06/02 /health/mini-meals-food-drayer/index.html.

"Email Statistics Report, 2015-2019." The Radicati Group, Inc. March 2015. www.radicati.com/wp/wp-content/uploads /2015/02/Email-Statistics-Report-2015-2019-Executive -Summary.pdf.

Food and Drug Administration. "Confused by Date Labels on Packaged Foods?" Accessed July 4, 2019. www.fda.gov /consumers/consumer-updates/confused-date-labels -packaged-foods.

Friedman, Zach. "Student Loan Debt Statistics In 2019: A $1.5 Trillion Crisis." *Forbes*. February 25, 2019. www.forbes.com/sites/zackfriedman/2019/02/25 /student-loan-debt-statistics-2019/#54e6fd8133fb.

Hoyle, Rhiannon and Rachel Pannett. "Marie Kondo Isn't Sparking Joy for Thrift Stores." *The Wall Street Journal.* March 6, 2019. www.wsj.com/articles/marie-kondo-persuaded-you-to -jettison-your-junk-thrift-stores-sayenough-11551889124.

Insurify. "SUV Ownership in America: Where Bigger Is Better." December 17, 2018. www.insurify.com/insights/suv -ownership-in-america-where-bigger-is-better/.

Johnson, Emma. "The Real Cost of Your Shopping Habits" *Forbes.* January 15, 2015. www.forbes.com/sites /emmajohnson/2015/01/15/the-real-cost-of-your -shopping-habits/#457c09e01452.

Kwiatkowski, Andreas. "Introducing the Eisenhower Matrix." *Eisenhower.* Accessed June 30, 2019. www.eisenhower.me /eisenhower-matrix/.

Leonhardt, Megan. "Here's How Much Debt Americans Have at Every Age." *CNBC.* August 20, 2018. www.cnbc.com /2018/08/20/how-much-debt-americans-have-at -every-age.html.

Moutray, Chad, Ph.D., CBE. "An Economic Analysis of the U.S. Cleaning Products Industry." *Center for Manufacturing Research.* September 27, 2018. www.cleaninginstitute.org /sites/default/files/assets/1/AssetManager/ACI_Report _ExecSum.pdf.

National Sleep Foundation, the. "Sleep Hygiene." Accessed June 27, 2019. www.sleepfoundation.org/articles /sleep-hygiene.

Ramsey, Dave. "6 Types of Shoppers: Which One Are You?" *Dave Ramsey*. Accessed July 4, 2019. www.daveramsey .com/blog/the-six-kinds-of-shoppers/.

Smith, Martin J. "Can You Buy a Better Self-Image?" *Insight by Stanford Business*. February 16, 2017. www.gsb.stanford .edu/insights/can-you-buy-better-self-image.

Tierney, John. "Do You Suffer from Decision Fatigue?" *The New York Times*. August 17, 2011. www.nytimes.com/2011/08/21 /magazine/do-you-suffer-from-decision-fatigue.html ?pagewanted=all.

United States Postal Service. "One Day in the Life of the U.S. Postal Service." Accessed June 25, 2019. https://facts.usps .com/one-day/.

U.S. Travel Association. "State of American Vacation 2018." May 8, 2018. www.ustravel.org/research/state-american -vacation-2018.

Wansink, Brian and Jeffery Sobal. "Mindless Eating: The 200 Daily Food Decisions We Overlook." *Environment and Behavior*, 39:1 (January 2007), 106-23. www.researchgate .net/publication/227344004_Mindless_Eating_The _200_Daily_Food_Decisions_We_Overlook.

Index

Acknowledgments

This has truly been an amazing experience. I never imagined I would have the opportunity to write a book on a topic I'm so passionate about, and I have many to thank for accomplishing this labor of love.

First, I would like to thank Life, who is the greatest teacher of all. Many of the strategies in this book come from my own personal experiences of striving for a simpler life. To that end, I must also show gratitude to my ancestors, without whom I would not exist and who are the original minimalists. I would also like to thank my mother, Althea Massey, to whom I also dedicated this book and whose support has been immeasurable throughout my whole life, but especially in the past six years.

Moving on to the Callisto team, I would like to thank Wesley Chui for his assistance and patience in securing this opportunity. To Lia Ottaviano, the managing editor on this project, thank you for your invaluable feedback and encouragement throughout this process. To Victoria DeRosa, the development editor, who also provided considerate queries and commentary—I'm appreciative of your efforts. I also know there are many people who worked behind the scenes to make this project come to life and I'm grateful for your labor. Lastly, I'd like to thank Callisto Media for making space and allowing me to add to the canon of resources on simplicity.

Finally, I want to offer my gratitude to the Black Minimalists team and community. To Farai and Kenya, your friendship, accountability, and contributions have helped me grow and refine my personhood. To the community, thank you for inspiring me daily and for your collective rallying as we struggle toward liberation through simplicity.

About the Author

 **Yolanda V Acree** has been coaching and writing about simple living for over five years via her personal blog, YolandaVAcree.com, and community site, BlackMinimalists.net. Her interest in minimalism was sparked by her own quest to simplify her life beginning in 2012. She is the author of e-guide *Live Simply & Be Free*, curator of and contributor to *Simply Black: Personal Essays by Black Minimalists*, and co-facilitates the *Black & Minimalist* e-course. You can find her sharing the simple things that inspire her on Instagram, @yolandavacree.